Workbook

ASSiMiL®

French

False beginners

Estelle Demontrond-Box

I0805550

About this workbook

The 20 lessons in this workbook, which contain some 200 exercises, will allow you to progressively review and practice the fundamentals of French, from pronunciation and vocabulary through to simple and more complex sentence construction.

Each lesson deals with a key grammatical point such as verb conjugation and usage, parts of speech and sentence structure, as well as giving pronunciation tips. The exercises allow active and contextual reinforcement of the points covered, calling upon your knowledge of the language. The aim of the workbook is to provide a fun and systematic way to consolidate your French skills.

As you work through the exercises, you can self-assess your results by selecting the appropriate icon after each exercise (🙂 if the majority of your answers were correct, 😐 if around half your answers were correct, or 🙁 if less than half were correct). After a lesson, enter the number of icons of each type you received in the exercises, and then enter these totals into the final score table at the end of the workbook so you can tally your final results after completing all the exercises.

Contents

1 Alphabet and pronunciation

The alphabet

The French alphabet is the same as the English alphabet, although the letters are pronounced differently:

A (ah)	G (zhay)	M (em)	S (es)	Y (eegrek)
B (bay)	H (ash)	N (en)	T (tay)	Z (zed)
C (say)	I (ee)	O (oh)	U (ew)	
D (day)	J (zhee)	P (pay)	V (vay)	
E (uh)	K (kah)	Q (kew)	W (doobluh vay)	
F (ef)	L (el)	R (er)	X (eeks)	

1 **Spell these words aloud using the French alphabet.**

B-O-N-J-O-U-R
(hello)

C-H-A-I-S-E
(chair)

M-A-M-A-N
(mum)

H-E-U-R-E-U-X
(happy [m.]*)*

Q-U-E-S-T-I-O-N

F-L-E-U-R
(flower)

R-A-V-I-E
(pleased [f.]*)*

V-R-A-I
(true [m.]*)*

G-E-N-T-I-L-L-E
(nice [f.]*)*

W-A-G-O-N

P-A-P-Y
(grandad)

Z-O-O

Written accents in French

French has a number of accents used for pronunciation or spelling reasons:

- An acute (**aigu**) accent **[é]** indicates that the vowel **[e]** should be pronounced *eh*.
- A grave (**grave**) accent **[è]** indicates that the vowel **[e]** should be pronounced *ay*, or is used with **[a]** or **[u]** to distinguish words that are otherwise spelled the same.
- A circumflex (**circonflexe**) accent **[â]** is used on any vowel to indicate the presence of a historical letter. It lengthens an **[a], [o]** or **[u]** vowel sound.
- A diaeresis (**le tréma**) **[ë]** is used to indicate that a vowel should be pronounced independently rather than blended with another vowel, as in **Noël** (*no-ehl*).
- A cedilla (**la cédille**) **[ç]** indicates that the **[c]** is pronounced *s* as in **ça**.

2 Using a French dictionary, add the correct accents or other marks to these words and then give their meaning.

E.g. frere → frère = brother

a. une mere → ____ = ______

b. peut-etre → __________ = _____

c. Noel → ____ = __________

d. une lecon → _____ = ______

e. le present → _______ = _______

f. tot → ___ = _____

g. un garcon → ______ = ___

h. le passe → _____ = ____

3 Underline the correct word in the following sentences.

a. Mon **pere / pêre / pére / père** est au travail.

b. Il me tarde d'être à **Noêl / Noél / Noël / Noèl** !

c. Pourriez-vous me donner des **glassons / glasons / glacons / glaçons**, s'il vous plaît ?

d. Oublie le **passe / passè / passé / passê**. Pense au futur !

e. Elles portent la **meme / mème / méme / même** robe !

Silent letters

Unfortunately, French is rarely pronounced as it is written. Certain letters are not pronounced at all!

- This often occurs at the end of words, such as
  – with **final consonants: salut** *hi [sahloo]*
  – with a **final [e]: femme** *woman [fam]*
- The letter **[h]** at the beginning of a word is always silent: **homme** *man [ohm]*.

4 Read these words with silent letters aloud and then write the English translation below each word.

froid	porc	trois	vous	abricot
....	....	....	....	....
chez	mot	chat	salut	outil
....	....	....	....	....
estomac	beaucoup	trop	nerf	deux
....	....	....	....	....

5 Place each word in the appropriate column according to whether or not it ends with a silent letter.

TURC POULE HIVER FOUR LOURD OURS FROID ŒUF

Silent final letter	Voiced final letter

Nasal vowels, the [u] and [r] sounds

- **Nasalized vowels:** In syllables ending with **[m]** or **[n]** (as in **tante** *aunt*, **oncle** *uncle*), the **[m]** or **[n]** are barely voiced, but they make the preceding vowel sound "nasal". The best way to approximate these sounds in English is to imagine a vowel followed by **[-ng]** (as in *song*) and stopping short before pronouncing the **-ng**.
- **The French [u]:** This tricky sound is not the English **[oo]**, but is closer to an **[ew]** sound. To imitate it, pronounce **[ee]** while pursing your lips with the tongue towards the front of the mouth, its tip resting against the lower teeth.
- **The French RRRRRRRRRRRRR!:** The **[r]** is the pet hate of most English speakers learning French. But with a bit of practice, it doesn't have to be! It is a guttural sound somewhere between an **[h]** and an **[r]**. It is close to the Spanish **[j]** or the Scottish **[ch]** in *Loch Ness*. To pronounce it, place the base of your tongue at the back of your throat and the tip of your tongue behind the lower teeth and make a sound as if you were coughing up a hairball!

Liaison

The letters **s, x, z, t, d, n** and **m**, which are normally silent at the end of a word, are sometimes pronounced if the following word starts with a **vowel sound** or a **mute [h]**, as in *les enfants [layz an^{g}fahn]*. Note that: not every **h** is mute, in some words, you briefly pause like in **haricot**, *bean*.

6 Practice your pronunciation by reading the following sentences aloud.

a. Tu es sûr que la poule est sur le mur ?

b. Où est ton chien ? Sur ou sous le banc ?

c. As-tu entendu ? Sa sœur a eu un garçon !

d. J'ai perdu le numéro de téléphone de sa tante.

7 Indicate whether or not there should be a liaison by ticking Y (✓) or N (✗).

	Y	N
un homme		
les élèves		
les haricots		

	Y	N
les vieux éléphants		
le petit ami		
les yeux		

8 Complete this crossword using words you have seen in this lesson.

Down

1. Polite form of “you”
4. A lot of
5. A word
6. The number 2
8. Man – mother
10. Very happy *(f.)*

Across

B. A greeting
C. A short conjunction
E. Informal greeting
G. The opposite of hot
H. A school student
I. Too much

9 Add the 10 missing accents in the text below.

« Mon pere est rentre hier soir du Venezuela pour feter Noel en famille. Il veut des festivites francaises ! C'est genial d'etre enfin ensemble ! C'est l'heure des cadeaux et des escargots ! Nous allons nous regaler ! Quelle fete cela sera ! »

Congratulations! You have completed Lesson 1! It is time to count up how many of each type of icon you received. Then record your results in the final self-assessment table on page 128.

2
Articles and nouns

French nouns

- In French, all nouns have a gender. They are either masculine (*m.*) or feminine (*f.*). Unfortunately, it is not easy to tell which gender a word is just from the way it is spelled. Typically a noun that ends in **[-e] (une fille)** is feminine, while a noun that ends in a consonant is masculine **(un garçon)**. However, there are a lot of exceptions (e.g. **un arbre)**. The only sure way to know the gender of a noun is to check in a dictionary. Always try to learn a new noun with its gender. Note also that nouns that refer to people often have a different masculine and feminine form, such as **un Américain** *an American man* and **une Américaine** *an American woman*.

- To form the plural (*pl.*) of most nouns, an **[-s]** is added (**une fille → des filles**). If the noun ends in **-u**, an **[-x]** is added (**un cheveu → des cheveux)**. If the noun ends in **-al**, an **[-aux]** is added (**un journal → des journaux**). If the noun ends in **-s**, **-x**, or **-z**, there is no change in the plural form (**le fils → les fils**).

1 Tick the right answer: are the following words masculine (M), feminine (F) or plural (P)?

Nouns	M	F	P
salon	☐	☐	☐
chambre	☐	☐	☐
toilettes	☐	☐	☐
cave	☐	☐	☐
grenier	☐	☐	☐
cuisine	☐	☐	☐

2 Complete the following table (using a dictionary if necessary).

Masculine singular	Feminine singular	Masculine plural
	une amie	
un Français		
		des marchands
un marié		
	une avocate	
		des invités

Definite articles

The definite article *the* has four forms in French. The form varies according to whether the noun it is used with is masculine, feminine, singular or plural:

- **le** before a masculine noun: **le père**
- **la** before a feminine noun: **la mère**
- **l'** before a singular noun starting with a vowel or a silent [h]: **l'enfant, l'hôtel**
- **les** before a plural noun: **les parents**

	Singular	Plural
Masculine	**le/l'**	**les**
Feminine	**la/l'**	**les**

3 Circle the correct definite article.

a. (Le / La / L' / Les) maison est grande !

b. (Le / La / L' / Les) filles sont très jolies !

c. (Le / La / L' / Les) enfants sont gentils.

d. (Le / La / L' / Les) eau est trop froide !

e. (Le / La / L' / Les) garçon joue au football.

f. (Le / La / L' / Les) homme est très grand !

4 Connect each noun to the correct definite article.

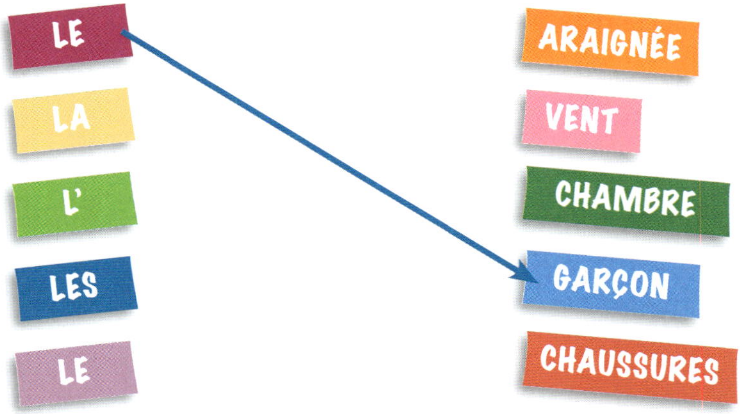

Indefinite articles

- **un** and **une** are the equivalent of the English article *a(n)*. The article **un** is used in front of a masculine noun (**un arbre** *a tree*) and **une** is used in front of a feminine noun (**une maison** *a house*).
- The article **des** is used in front of a plural noun: **des frères** *brothers*.

	Singular	Plural
Masculine	**un**	**des**
Feminine	**une**	**des**

5 Circle the correct indefinite article. You can use a dictionary to check if the noun is feminine or masculine.

a. Il y a **(un / une / des)** chat sur le toit.
b. As-tu **(un / une / des)** crayons dans ta trousse ?
c. Je mange **(un / une / des)** gâteaux tous les jours.
d. Il veut **(un / une / des)** guitare pour Noël.
e. Nous avons **(un / une / des)** chien.

Saying *some* & *any*

In French, articles that refer to an indeterminate quantity (for example, in reference to food) must be included before a noun. The equivalent *some* or *any* in English can sometimes be omitted, but the article is ALWAYS required in French (*I have money. / I have some money.* = **J'ai de l'argent.**)

There are four forms:

- **du** before a masculine noun: **du café**
- **de la** before a feminine noun: **de la salade**
- **de l'** before a singular noun starting with a vowel or a silent [h]: **de l'eau**
- **des** before a plural noun: **des biscuits**

	Singular	Plural
Masculine	**du / de l'**	**des**
Feminine	**de la / de l'**	**des**

6 **Order your pizza using the right articles from the pizza box!**

« Garçon, s'il vous plaît ! Je voudrais .... pizza avec .... champignons, ... jambon et .... sauce tomate. Je veux .... pizza rapidement car j'ai très faim ! J'aimerais aussi .... eau ! Merci ! »

de la   une   la   de l'   du   des

Indefinite articles in the negative or with an adjective

- As a general rule, if an indefinite article is used with a negative verb, **un**, **une**, **du**, **de la**, **de l'**, **des** are replaced by **de** or **d'**. **J'ai une voiture. → Je n'ai pas de voiture. J'ai des amis. → Je n'ai pas d'amis.**
- If an adjective is placed before a plural noun, **des** is usually replaced by **de**: **J'ai des chaussettes. → J'ai de jolies chaussettes.**

7 Make the following sentences negative.

a. Tu as un jardin.

....

b. Nous avons des enfants.

....

c. Ils ont de gentils parents.

....

d. J'ai une maison.

....

e. Elles ont des amis.

....

Feminine or masculine nouns: people and jobs

- The gender of nouns referring to people and animals is easy. For a male, **un** or **le** is used with the masculine form of the noun. For a female, **une** or **la** is used: **un homme** *a man* – **une femme** *a woman*; **le père** *the father* – **la mère** *the mother*; **le chat** *the cat* (male) – **la chatte** *the cat* (female).
- In general, the feminine form of a noun is made by adding an **-e** to the masculine noun: **un avocat / une avocate** *lawyer.* But some endings undergo a more drastic change (**-er** → **-ère**; **-en** → **-enne**; **-an** → **-anne**; **-on** → **-onne**; **-eur** → **-euse**; **-eur** → **-rice**; **-at** → **-atte**; **-f** → **-ve**; **-x** → **-se**). And some nouns, especially referring to occupations, can refer to either a male or a female: **un/une docteur**, **un/une élève**.

8 **Match each occupation with its English equivalent.**

un avocat •	• a waiter
un chanteur •	• a singer
un professeur •	• a writer
un serveur •	• a lawyer
un concierge •	• an engineer
un écrivain •	• a caretaker
un ingénieur •	• a teacher

9 **With the help of a dictionary, find the masculine or feminine term for the following nouns.**

Masculine	Feminine	Masculine	Feminine
un vendeur	....	un maître	....
....	une musicienne	un paysan	....
un acteur	....	....	une secrétaire
....	une boulangère	un dentiste	....
....	une étudiante	un professeur	....

Well done! You have reached the end of Lesson 2! Count up the icons for the exercises and record your result in the final evaluation table on page 128.

3
Pronouns
(a pronoun is used to replace a noun)

Subject pronouns

- The subject in a clause is the person or thing that performs the action described by the verb. To avoid repeating the same word, a subject pronoun is often used to replace the noun in subsequent references:
  Gaston aime les frites. → Il aime les frites.
- The French subject pronouns are as follows:

SINGULAR		PLURAL	
je/j'	*I*	**nous**	*we*
tu	*you* (informal)	**vous**	*you* (plural / formal singular)
il	*he, it* (m.)	**ils**	*they* (m.)
elle	*she, it* (f.)	**elles**	*they* (f.)
on	*one*		

- Note that:
  - **je** becomes **j'** in front of a vowel or a silent **h** (e.g. **J'ai un frère.**)
  - **tu** and **vous** both mean *you*, however, **tu** is informal and is used when talking to a friend, a family member or someone close. When speaking to more than one person or to a stranger or in any situation that requires polite address, **vous** is used.
  - **il/elle** and **ils/elles** can refer to inanimate objects, animals or people. They need to agree in gender and number with the noun they replace. However, **ils** is used if a group includes both genders.
  - **on** means *one* but is often used in the sense of 'you' or 'people', or instead of **nous** to mean *we*.

1 **Translate the English subject pronouns below into French.**

a. *(You* [sing. inf.]*)* .... es très grande !

b. *(She)* .... a quarante-cinq ans.

c. *(We)* .... sommes canadiens.

d. *(They* [f.]*)*.......................... adorent les araignées !

e. *(You* [pl.]*)*.......................... êtes très élégantes !

2 **Fill in the blanks using the appropriate subject pronoun from the gift box below.**

a. .... sont au Kenya.

b. .... êtes au cinéma ?

c. .... est heureuse.

d. .... sommes à la boulangerie.

e. .... suis allergique au pollen.

The verbs *être* (to be) & *avoir* (to have) in the present tense

Here are the subject pronouns for each person with the useful verbs **être** and **avoir**.

être		avoir	
I am	**je suis**	*I have*	**j'ai**
you are (singular informal)	**tu es**	*you have* (singular informal)	**tu as**
he is / it is (m.)	**il est**	*he has / it has* (m.)	**il a**
she is / it is (f.)	**elle est**	*she has / it has* (f.)	**elle a**
we are	**nous sommes**	*we have*	**nous avons**
you are (plural/formal)	**vous êtes**	*you have* (plural/formal)	**vous avez**
they are (m.) (f.)	**ils sont** **elles sont**	*they have* (m.) (f.)	**ils ont** **elles ont**

3 Complete the following sentences using the correct form of be (*être*).

a. Il .... peintre.

b. Nous .... étudiants.

c. Elles .... actrices.

d. Vous .... boulangers ?

e. Je .... traducteur.

4 Complete the following sentences using the correct form of have (*avoir*).

a. J'....................................... 45 ans.

b. Nous .... un chien.

c. Ils .... 3 vélos.

d. Tu .... une moto ?

e. Elle .... 2 maisons.

5 Complete the following sentences using the correct form of either be (*être*) or have (*avoir*).

a. Philippe .... ingénieur.

b. Karine .... un chien et deux hamsters.

c. Clémentine .... très jolie.

d. Nicolas .... gentil.

e. Oriane .... une belle robe.

6 Underline the correct subject pronoun.

a. Il / Elle / Tu
est courageuse.

b. Vous / Tu / J'
avez une belle voiture !

c. Il / Vous / Nous
sommes en Australie.

d. Elles / Ils / Vous
sont petits.

e. Je / Il / Tu
suis belge.

Direct object pronouns

- The direct object in a clause directly receives the action of the verb. In French, direct object pronouns are placed in front of the verb: **Xavier <u>me</u> voit.** *Xavier sees <u>me</u>.*

- The direct object pronouns are:

ENGLISH	FRENCH
me	**me/m'**
you (sing. inf.)	**te/t'**
him/it (m.)	**le/l'**
her/it (f.)	**la/l'**
us	**nous**
you (plural/formal)	**vous**
them	**les**

- **m'**, **t'**, **l'** are used when the pronoun comes before a verb starting with a vowel or a silent **h**.

- Don't forget to use the appropriate pronoun for *you* depending on the context: singular informal (**te**), singular formal (**vous**) or plural (**vous**). Also remember that even when referring to inanimate objects, the gender of the noun is reflected in the pronoun (**le** or **la**).

7 Complete the following sentences, using the appropriate direct object pronoun.

a. Je .... aime ! *(her)*

b. Tu .... attends quelques minutes ? *(me)*

c. Elles .... ont invités au restaurant. *(us)*

d. Je .... ai vus au cinéma. *(you* [pl.]*)*

e. Stéphanie .... attend depuis une heure. *(you* [singular informal]*)*

8 Underline the correct answer. Two answers are sometimes possible!

a. Marc le prend tous les jours. ➜ **le train / la voiture**

b. Il l'adore ! ➜ **Maéva / Bruno**

c. Tu la ranges dans quel tiroir ? ➜ **la fourchette / le couteau**

d. Elle les voit tous les week-ends. ➜ **ses cousins / ses cousines**

e. Il vous comprend très bien. ➜ **toi et ton amie / Adèle et Catherine**

Indirect object pronouns

- The indirect object pronouns are:

ENGLISH	FRENCH
me	**me/m'**
you (sing. inf.)	**te/t'**
him	**lui**
her	**lui**
us	**nous**
you (plural/formal)	**vous**
them	**leur**

- An indirect object indirectly receives the action of the verb. Frequently this is a person that the action is directed 'to' or 'at'. (Note that some French verbs take indirect objects that would be direct objects in English.) Verbs that require indirect objects usually refer to giving, telling, offering or showing: verbs that convey that something is done to or for someone.
  Sophie parle à Jérôme. *Sophie speaks to Jerome.* → **Sophie lui parle.** *Sophie speaks to him.*

Sophie	**parle**	**à**	**Jérôme**
subject	*verb = action*	*preposition*	*noun*
Sophie	**lui**	**parle**	
subject	*indirect object = replaces Jérôme*	*verb = action*	

9 Complete these sentences using the appropriate indirect object pronoun.

a. Il a dit bonjour à Sophie. ➜ Il .... a dit bonjour.

b. J'ai donné une lettre à toi et à ton frère. ➜ Je...................... ai donné une lettre.

c. Marie pose une question à toi et à moi. ➜ Marie .... pose une question.

d. Elle téléphone à son père tous les dimanches. ➜ Elle .... téléphone tous les dimanches.

e. Ton père a répondu (à toi). ➜ Ton père.. a répondu.

10 Direct or indirect object? Fill in the crossword by completing the sentences below with the appropriate object pronoun.

1→ Il .... *(her)* a répondu oui !

2→ Je .... *(you* [plural]*)* ai écrit une lettre.

3→ Vous ......*(us)* indiquez la mauvaise direction !

4→ Tu .... *(us)* parles trop fort !

5→ Angèle .... *(them)* chante une chanson.

6→ Je .... *(her)* vois dans la cuisine.

7→ Elles ..... *(him)* racontent une longue histoire.

8→ Marcelle veut ....*(you* [formal]*)* voir.

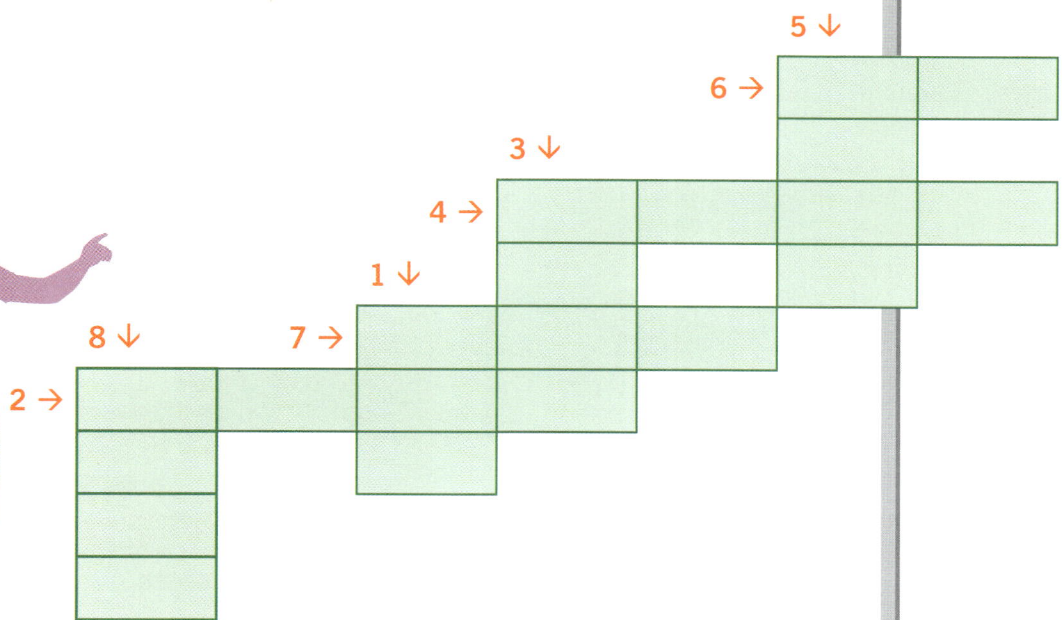

Très bien ! You have reached the end of Lesson 3! Count up the icons for each exercise and record your results here and in the table on page 128.

4 Adjectives

Descriptive adjectives

- An adjective is a word used to describe a noun or a pronoun. In French, unlike in English, adjectives must agree in gender (feminine or masculine) and number (singular or plural) with the nouns that they modify.
- Most adjectives have four possible forms:

	Singular	Plural
Masculine	joli	jolis
Feminine	jolie	jolies

- To form the feminine of an adjective, you usually add an **[-e]** to its masculine form: **joli → jolie**. However, some forms are irregular:
  - If the masculine form already ends with an **[e]**, then it does not change in the feminine: **Il est triste. → Elle est triste.**
  - Some other ways that a masculine adjective can change to a feminine form include:

    [-n] → [-nne]
    [-c] → [-que]
    [-l] → [-lle]
    [-er] → [-ère]
    [-et] → [-ète]
    [-et] → [-ette]
    [-eur] → [-euse]
    [-eur] → [-rice]
    [-f] → [-ve]
    [-c]/[-s] → [-che]
    [-g] → [-gue]
    [-x] → [-se]
    [-u] → [-üe]

  - For some adjectives, the feminine form is different altogether (**vieux → vieille; fou → folle**). You will just need to learn these over time!
- To form a plural adjective, **[-s]** is usually added to the singular: **joli → jolis**.
  - If the singular form already ends in **[-s]** or **[-x]**, then it remains the same.
  - If its singular form is **[-al]**, then it usually changes to **[-aux]**.
  - If it is **[-eau]**, it changes to **[-eaux]**.

1 Complete the following table.

Masculine singular	Feminine singular	Masculine plural	Feminine plural
français	française	....	françaises
....	mexicaine	mexicains	mexicaines
grand	grande	grands	....
gros	grosse	....	grosses
poli	....	polis	polies
beau	belle	beaux	....
bon	....	bons	bonnes
....	vieille	vieux	vieilles

2 Fill in the blanks in the following sentences by choosing the appropriate adjective.

patient *méchants* *gentille*
amoureux *maladroits* *bavardes*

a. Quelle générosité ! Elle est vraiment très .... !

b. Fais très attention. Ces chiens sont ....

c. Sois .... Sébastien. Ton tour viendra !

d. Regarde ces deux femmes là-bas ! Elles sont vraiment .... !

e. Oh Marceau, avec un tel sourire, toi, tu es .... !

f. Ils sont tellement .... ! Ils cassent toujours quelque chose...

- Although in English adjectives usually come before the noun that they modify, in French most adjectives come after the noun that they describe:

  a blue house
  → **une maison bleue.**

- Some adjectives, however, come before the noun, such as:

  – cardinal numbers
  – **beau, bon, court, dernier, gentil, grand, gros, haut, jeune, joli, long, mauvais, nouveau, petit** and **vieux.**

3 Place the adjective in the right place in the following sentences.

a. Oh, regarde ! Quel paysage ! **(beau)**

....

b. J'aime beaucoup cette robe. **(rouge)**

....

c. C'est une fille. **(jalouse)**

....

d. Quel tableau ! **(joli)**

....

e. Je suis fatigué. C'était un voyage. **(long)**

....

Nationalities

- When talking about someone from a particular country (i.e. when the nationality is used as a noun), a capital letter is used: **un Australien / les Australiens**.
- However, if you are describing someone or something (i.e. when the nationality is an adjective), it is lower case: **la cuisine française**; **les enfants sont anglais**.
- The form changes for gender: **un Africain / une Africaine**.
- Note that the names of countries also have a gender in French: *Finland* = **La Finlande**.

4 Underline the correct form of these adjectives showing nationality.

a. Mon ami est anglais / anglaise / anglaises.

b. Cette fille est coréen / coréenne / coréennes.

c. Ses parents sont finlandais / finlandaise / finlandaises.

d. Ce groupe de musique est canadien / canadienne / canadiens / canadiennes.

e. Les joueurs de cette équipe sont chinois / chinoise / chinoises.

f. Les chanteuses de cette chorale sont américain / américaine / américains / américaines.

5 Fill in the following table.

Flags	Masc. sing.	Fem. sing.	Masc. pl.	Fem. pl.
	Hollandais	Hollandaise	Hollandais	Hollandaises
	....	....	....	....
	....	....	....	....
	....	....	....	....
	....	....	....	....
	....	....	....	....
	....	....	....	....
	....	....	....	....
	....	....	....	....
	....	....	....	....

Colours

Most colour adjectives also have four forms, apart from:
– those named after foods, flowers, gems or metals (**cerise, lavande, argent,** etc.)
– compound forms (**bleu marine**).

These do not change in the feminine or the plural: **Ses chaussures sont marron** (*brown*, 'chestnut'). **Elle a des yeux bleu clair** (*light blue*).

6 Fill in the following table.

Colours	Masc. sing.	Fem. sing.	Masc. pl.	Fem. pl.
	jaune	jaune	jaunes	jaunes
	....	....	....	....
	....	....	....	....
	....	....	....	....
	....	....	....	....
	....	....	....	....
	....	....	....	....
	....	....	....	....
	....	....	....	....
	....	....	....	....
	....	....	....	....

7 Write the correct form of the adjective in the following sentences.

a. De belles chaussures (bleu)
....

b. De très jolies fleurs (jaune)
....

c. De beaux pulls (marron)
....

d. Une élégante cravate (noir)
....

e. Un buisson (vert)
....

Demonstrative adjectives

- Demonstrative adjectives (*this, these*) point out someone or something. In French, they need to agree in both gender and number with the noun they refer to.

	Singular	Plural
Masculine	ce / cet	ces
Feminine	cette	ces

- The form **cet** is used in front of a masculine singular noun or adjective beginning with a vowel or a silent **[h]**: **cet ananas** *this pineapple*, **cet habit** *this piece of clothing*.

8 Circle the correct form.

a. J'ai beaucoup aimé (**ce / cet / cette / ces**) film !

b. Quelle horreur ! (**Ce / Cet / Cette / Ces**) pomme était pourrie *(rotten)* !

c. (**Ce / Cet / Cette / Ces**) enfants sont très bruyants *(noisy)*.

d. Peux-tu me passer (**ce / cet / cette / ces**) plat, s'il te plaît ?

e. (**Ce / Cet / Cette / Ces**) homme a une cravate rigolote !

Possessive adjectives

- Possessive adjectives (*my, your, his, her, our, their*) in French must agree in gender and number with what is possessed, NOT with the possessor.

masc. sing.	fem. sing.	plural
mon	ma	mes
ton	ta	tes
son	sa	ses
notre	notre	nos
votre	votre	vos
leur	leur	leurs

- Note that the masculine form is used before a word that starts with a vowel or a silent **h** even if it is a feminine noun: **mon amie Sophie, mon histoire**.

9 **Select the appropriate possessive adjective from the previous table for each of the following sentences:**

a. As-tu vu .... *(my)* livre ? Je ne le trouve pas !

b. .... *(his)* sœurs sont très grandes !

c. J'adore .... *(their)* chien ! Il est très amusant !

d. .... *(his)* amie s'appelle Éléanore.

e. .... *(your)* père est très gentil, Anne!

With parts of the body

When talking about parts of the body, a definite article is used instead of a possessive adjective:

J'ai <u>les</u> cheveux blonds.
I have blond hair.

Elle s'est lavé <u>les</u> mains.
She washed her hands.

10 **Translate the following sentences.**

a. He has brown hair.

....

b. His father is French.

....

c. Their cat is white.

....

d. She washed her hair yesterday.

....

e. Your *(pl.)* house is very big!

....

Great! You have reached the end of Lesson 4! Now count up the icons for each exercise and record your results here and on page 128.

5

Comparatives and superlatives

Making comparisons

There are three ways to compare two things or people.

- To express inferiority, you use: **moins … que …** *less … than …*
  (e.g. **Karine est <u>moins</u> fatiguée <u>que</u> Coralie.** *Karine is less tired than Coralie.*)
- To express equality, you use: **aussi … que …** *as … as …*
  (e.g. **Sophie est <u>aussi</u> jolie <u>qu'</u>Éloïse.** *Sophie is as pretty as Éloïse.*)
- To express superiority, you use: **plus … que** *more … than …*
  (e.g. **Pierre est <u>plus</u> bavard <u>que</u> Daniel.** *Pierre is more talkative than Daniel.*)

Note that **que** becomes **qu'** in front of vowels or a silent **h** and don't forget that an adjective must agree with what it describes (i.e. the first of the two items compared).

1 Turn the words in brackets into comparative adjectives following the symbols shown (− inferiority; = equality; + superiority).

E.g. Mon frère est (grand +) <u>plus grand</u> que mon père.

a. Son chat est (rapide −) .... son chien !

b. Floriane est (jolie =) .... Martine.

c. Ce livre est (intéressant +) .... celui-là.

d. Laurent est (gentil −) .... Sylvain.

e. Ta maison est (grande =) .... la mienne.

2 Translate the following sentences into English.

a. Cette table est plus grande que celle-là *(that one).*

= ....

b. Alexandre est aussi sportif que Julien.

= ....

c. Sophie est moins jolie que Karine.

= ....

d. Julien est aussi drôle que Lily.

= ....

e. Le sac bleu est plus grand que le sac noir.

= ....

3 In the following sentences, underline the correct form of the adjective.

a. Elles sont plus **bavard / bavarde / bavards / bavardes** que nous.

b. Marion est aussi **beau / belle / beaux / belles** que Sophie.

c. Mathieu est aussi **intelligent / intelligente / intelligents / intelligentes** que Claire.

d. Louis et Gabriel sont moins **gentil / gentille / gentils / gentilles** que Catherine et Jennifer.

e. L'arbre de droite est plus **petit / petite / petits / petites** que l'arbre de gauche.

Adverbs

- An adverb typically modifies a verb (e.g. **Il écrit lentement.** = *He writes slowly.*) To make a comparison using an adverb, the same rules apply as for adjectives (see previous page).
- Common adverbs include **vite** *quickly*, **bien** *well* and **mal** *badly*. Adverbs can also be formed from adjectives.
  - The usual way to form an adverb from an adjective is by adding the suffix **-ment** to the feminine form of the adjective (**seul** → **seule** → **seulement**).
  - There are also some irregular adverbs such as:
    prudent *careful* → **prudemment** *carefully*
    énorme *enormous* → **énormément** *enormously*
    meilleur *better* → **mieux** *better*
    gentil *nice* → **gentiment** *nicely*.

4 Adjective or adverb? Put the words in the correct column.

Adjectives	Adverbs

FACILEMENT belle rapidement

gentil mieux malheureusement

5 **Turn the following adjectives into adverbs.**
E.g. heureux → heureusement

a. rare → ....

b. poli → ....

c. courageux → .... → ....

d. prudent → ....

e. parfait → .... → ....

The superlative

- The superlative expresses the concept of *the most* or *the least* (typically expressed with the suffix *-est* in English). To form this, use the appropriate definite article **le, la** or **les** with **plus** or **moins** + adjective.
- Like all adjectives, superlative adjectives need to agree in gender and number with the noun they refer to (e.g. **Les pommes les plus vertes**.)
- Note that when the adjective comes after the noun, the article (**le, la** or **les**) is repeated (e.g. **C'est le restaurant le plus cher de la ville.**)
- Also, after a superlative, **de** is used to express 'in': *Julian is the most intelligent in the class.* = **Julian est le plus intelligent de la classe**.

6 **Circle the appropriate article in the following sentences.**

a. C'est le / la / les plus belle maison du quartier.

b. Ce sont les garçons le / la / les plus polis de la classe !

c. Ce sont le / la / les robes les plus laides du magasin.

d. C'est le / la / les chien le plus méchant du quartier.

e. C'est le / la / les fille la plus jolie du village.

7 **Put each superlative adjective into the correct form.**

a. Ces fleurs sont les plus **(coloré)** .... du jardin.

b. Elle est la plus **(active)** .... de sa classe.

c. Ce bébé est le plus **(mignon)** .... que je connaisse.

d. Leurs voitures sont les plus **(propre)** .... de la rue !

e. Jeanne est la femme la plus **(maladroit)** .... que je connaisse !

8 Insert the appropriate article or the preposition *de*.

a. C'est la maison .... plus chère du quartier.

b. Sophie est la fille .... moins sportive du groupe.

c. Jonathan est le garçon le plus rapide .... son club.

d. Les dattes sont les fruits .... plus sucrés.

e. Joséphine est la plus maligne .... l'école.

Irregular forms

- The superlative is more often used with adjectives, but can also be used with adverbs.
- The comparative of **mauvais** *bad* is **pire** *worse* and not **plus mauvais***:

* incorrect form

Il est pire que moi. = *He is worse than me.*

- It becomes **le pire** in the superlative: **C'est la pire semaine de ma vie !** = *It is the worst week of my life!*
- The comparative of the adjective **bon** *good* is **meilleur** *better*.
- The comparative of the adverb **bien** *well* is **mieux** *better* and the superlative is **le mieux** *the best*.

9 In the following sentences, write the appropriate comparative or superlative form.

E.g. Noah est (+ mignon) le plus mignon de sa classe.

a. Élisa est **(= étourdie)** .... Vanessa.

b. C'est (**+ bon)** .... gâteau du menu.

c. Ils sont **(+ timides)** .... leurs parents.

d. Audrey est la fille **(+ généreuse)** .... que je connaisse.

e. Ce livre est **(- mauvais)** .... que j'aie jamais lu !

Super ! You have completed Lesson 5! Now count up the icons for each exercise and record your results here and in the table on page 128.

6
Sentences and word order

Sentence structure

The most common word order in a French sentence is:
subject + verb + complement

Je	regarde	un film de science-fiction.
subject	*verb*	*complement*

1 Place the parts of the sentence in the right column.
E.g. Je vais au cinéma.

a. Il mange du gâteau.

b. Nous avons vu Charles et Simon.

c. Vous chantez une belle mélodie.

d. Elle donne des bonbons !

e. Nous aimons les films de science-fiction.

	Subject	Verb	Complement
	Je	vais	au cinéma.
a.			
b.			
c.			
d.			
e.			

2 **Put the elements into order to form sentences.**
E.g. suis / France / Je / en /. → Je suis en France.

a. au restaurant / a invité / Julie / ses amis /.

....

b. voiture / une / Sylvain / nouvelle / a acheté /.

....

c. Son / très / est / pull / joli /.

....

d. en / voyage / train / Christian / souvent /.

....

e. à 8 heures / prend / Léon / petit / son / déjeuner /.

....

Negative sentences

- Some of the most common negative constructions are **ne** + verb + any of the following:
  - **pas** *not*: **Nous n'avons pas de chien.** *We don't have a dog.*
  - **rien** *nothing, not anything*: **Je ne sais rien.** *I don't know anything.*
  - **plus** *no longer, no more*: **Solène ne boude plus.** *Solène is no longer sulking.*
  - **aucun/aucune** *none, not any*: **Il n'a aucun ami.** *He doesn't have any friends.*
  - **jamais** *never*: **Je ne suis jamais allé en Belgique.** *I have never been to Belgium.*
  - **ni … ni …** *neither … nor*: **Elle n'aime ni les pommes ni les poires.** *She likes neither apples nor pears.*
- Note that **ne** becomes **n'** before a vowel or a silent **h**. **Il n'habite pas chez ses parents.**
- In the perfect tenses (which are formed with the auxiliary verbs **avoir** or **être**), the auxiliary verb (rather than the main verb) is made negative (except with **ne … personne** and **ne … que**): **Il n'a jamais vu ce film.** *He has never seen this movie.*

3 Fill in the blanks with the appropriate negative construction.

E.g. Je ..... ai ...... de voiture. (not) → Je n'ai pas de voiture.

a. Estelle ...... est .... malade. **(not any longer)**

b. Martine .... a .... chat ...... chien. **(neither...nor)**

c. Stéphanie .... est....... méchante. **(not)**

d. Roger .... a .... mangé de calamar. **(never)**

e. Julian .... a .... bu hier soir. **(nothing)**

4 Turn the following statements into negative sentences.

a. Achille aime les fraises.

→ ....

b. Violette joue au tennis.

→ ....

c. Romain est blond.

→ ....

d. Séverine adore les films d'aventure.

→ ....

e. Olivier est petit.

→ ....

Forming questions

- To form a direct question, the subject and the verb can be inverted but do not have to be. **Es-tu content ? = Tu es content ?** *Are you happy?*
- If they are inverted and the subject is **il/elle/on** and the verb ends in a vowel, a **-t-** is added: **A-t-elle un chat ?**
- The formula **Est-ce que ... ?** can be put in front of the subject to form a direct question: **Est-ce que tu es content ?** *Are you happy?*

5 Put the elements into order to form sentences.

E.g. suis / France / je / en / Est-ce que / ?
→ Est-ce que je suis en France ?

a. les poires / Ginette / Est-ce que / aime / ?

→ ....

b. le chinois / elle / parle / Françoise / -t- / ?

→ ....

c. Australie / que / Marine / Est / en / ? / -ce / vit

→ ....

d. voir / Peut / venir / -il / me / ?

→ ....

e. -elle / mon / écouter / Veut / CD / ?

→ ....

6 Turn the statements into questions using *Est-ce que*.

E.g. Elle aime le gâteau. → Est-ce qu'elle aime le gâteau ?

a. Il déteste les chats.

→ .... ?

b. Tu vas au cinéma.

→ .... ?

c. Vous regardez la télé.

→ .... ?

d. Ils sont allés en Italie.

→ .... ?

e. Elle aime ma confiture.

→ .... ?

Question words

- Questions can also be formed using question words to ask for specific information. **Où vas-tu ?** *Where are you going?* – **Je vais au cinéma.** *I am going to the cinema.*
- If the question is negative, just put **ne** in front of the verb and **pas** after it. **Ne** becomes **n'** in front of a vowel or a silent **h**. E.g. **Ne mangez-vous pas de tarte ?** *Don't you eat pie?* **N'aimez-vous pas l'opéra ?** *Don't you like opera?*

Question words *(Les mots interrogatifs)*:

ENGLISH	FRENCH	ENGLISH	FRENCH
Who?	**Qui ?**	*Where?*	**Où ?**
With whom?	**Avec qui ?**	*Why?*	**Pourquoi ?**
What?	**Que ?** **Qu'est-ce que ?** **Quoi ?**	*How?*	**Comment ?**
		How much? / How many?	**Combien ?**
Which?	**Quel/Quelle/Quels/ Quelles ?**	*How long?*	**Combien de temps ?**
When?	**Quand ?**	*At what time?*	**À quelle heure ?**

7 Fill in the blanks with the appropriate question word.

a. .... son train arrive-t-il à la gare ?

b. .... a mangé mon yaourt ?

c. .... ce collier coûte-t-il ?

d. .... es-tu rentré ? Tu avais oublié la clé !

e. .... fait-il dans sa chambre ?

8 Form the question corresponding to the answer.

E.g. Quand viens-tu me voir ?
→ Tu viens me voir vendredi.

a. .... ?
→ Je vais bien merci !

b. .... ?
→ Il habite à Paris.

c. .... ?
→ Le film a duré 110 minutes.

d. .... ?
→ Sophie est rentrée parce qu'elle était fatiguée.

e. .... ?
→ C'est Louis qui a cassé le vase.

Differences between English and French

- Adjectives generally come after the noun in French: **Elle porte une robe verte.** *She is wearing a green dress.*
- Adverbs usually come after the verb: **Il ne va jamais en Italie.** *He never goes to Italy.*

9 Translate the following sentences.

a. I never go to the theatre. ➜ ....

b. Who took my book? ➜ ....

c. When is she coming back home? ➜ ....

d. I prefer the blue trousers. ➜ ....

e. He doesn't want to go out tonight. ➜ ....

10 Fill in the following telephone conversation using what you have learned in this lesson.

« Allô, Louise ? __ es-tu ?
Nous sommes inquiets. Nous __ savons (know)
___ où tu es. _________ ___
tu fais ? ________ n'as-tu pas téléphoné ?
__ recommence ______ (never) ! »

Excellent ! You have completed Lesson 6! It is time to count up the icons for the exercises and record your result here and in the table on page 128.

7

More on pronouns

Reflexive verbs, possessive pronouns, interrogative and relative pronouns

Reflexive pronouns

A reflexive verb (e.g. **se lever, se coucher, s'aimer**) includes a pronoun that must be included in its conjugations. The pronoun refers either to the subject of the verb (e.g. *oneself*) or can mean *each other*: **Ils s'aiment.** *They love each other.*

ENGLISH	FRENCH
myself	**me/m'**
yourself (informal)	**te/t'**
himself/itself	**se/s'**
herself/itself	**se/s'**
ourselves	**nous**
yourselves (*yourself*, formal)	**vous**
themselves	**se**

The pronoun is required in French.
He washes ('himself') *every morning.*
→ **Il se lave tous les matins.**

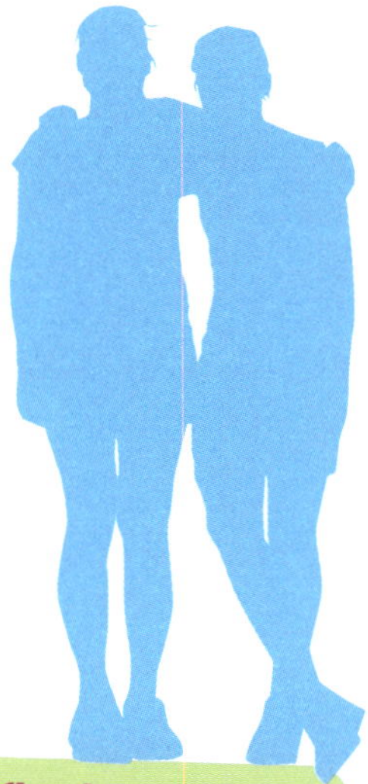

Reflexive verbs

These are verbs in which the subject and the object are the same. **Je me présente.** *I introduce myself.* They are common in French, though rare in English. They form the perfect tense with **être**.

se nous s' vous te me

1 Fill in the blanks using these reflexive pronouns. Beware! There is one too many!

a. Elle .... réveille à 7 heures tous les matins.

b. Je .... souviens de Bruno.

c. Nous .... sommes encore disputés.

d. Vous .... téléphonez souvent ?

e. Il ne .... est pas rasé ce matin.

2 **Fill in the blanks using the reflexive verb given.**

a. Elle .... très tôt le mardi matin. **(se lever)**

b. Je .... toujours en jean ! **(s'habiller)**

c. Il ne .... jamais. Quelle horreur ! **(se laver)**

d. Nous .... beaucoup ! Vive les vacances ! **(s'amuser)**

e. Vous .... à quelle heure le samedi soir ? **(se coucher)**

This one, that one, etc.

Demonstrative pronouns *(this, that, these, those)* replace a noun and must agree with its gender and number:

	Singular	**Plural**
Masculine	celui	ceux
Feminine	celle	celles

These pronouns are used either:

- With a preposition such as **à, de, dans** + noun: **J'aime cette maison mais je n'aime pas <u>celle</u> de mes parents.** ('I like this house, but I don't like that of my parents.')
- With a relative pronoun such as **qui**: **Celui <u>qui</u> est venu hier.** *The one who came yesterday.*
- With **-ci** *here* and **-là** *there* (placed after the pronoun):

	Masculine	**Feminine**	
Singular	celui-ci	celle-ci	*this one*
	celui-là	celle-là	*that one*
Plural	ceux-ci	celles-ci	*these ones*
	ceux-là	celles-là	*those ones*

- **ce** (or **c'** before a vowel) is the neutral form of **celui**. It is used in front of a relative pronoun (**ce que/ce qui**) and in the expression **c'est**.
- **ceci** and **cela** (abbreviated to **ça**): *this* and *that*. **<u>Cela</u> n'est pas vrai.** *That is not true*. These pronouns do not change in number and gender.

3 **Match each noun with its corresponding demonstrative pronoun.**

les montres	**celles**
l'enfant	**celui**
la chambre	**ceux**
les jupes	**celles**
le manteau	**celui**
les livres	**celle**

4 **Write the correct form of the pronoun given.**
E.g. J'adore ces boucles d'oreilles. Lesquelles ? → Celles-là (*those*).

a. Je veux voir ce film. Lequel ? → .... *(this one)*

b. J'aimerais une baguette, s'il vous plaît. Laquelle ? → .... *(this one)*

c. As-tu lu les livres de Bernard Werber ? Lesquels ? → .... *(those)*

d. As-tu amené le dossier ? Lequel ? → .... *(that one)*

e. Nous voulons visiter beaucoup de pays. Lesquels ? → .... *(these)*

Interrogative pronouns

- **Qui ?** is the question word that means *Who/Whom?*
- **Que ?** means *What?*
- **Quel ?** *Which?* or *What?* This is an adjective that needs to agree with the noun it refers to: **Quel jour ?** *What day?* **Quelle voiture ?** *Which car?* **Quels livres ?** *Which books?* **Quelles couleurs ?** *What colours?*

	Singular	Plural
Masculine	quel	quels
Feminine	quelle	quelles

- **Lequel ?** *Which one?* is the pronoun form of **quel**. It also needs to agree with the noun it refers to:

	Singular	Plural
Masculine	lequel	lesquels
Feminine	laquelle	lesquelles

5 ***QUI* or *QUE*? Choose the appropriate interrogative pronoun.**

a. .... fais-tu dans la cuisine ?

b. .... a pris mon manteau ?

c. .... veut-il faire ce soir ?

d. .... est ce jeune homme ?

e. .... a apporté le gâteau ?

6 **Fill in the blanks using the words given. Beware! There is an extra!**

quelles *quel* *lequel* *quelle* *laquelle* *lesquelles*

« .... robe veux-tu mettre aujourd'hui ?
– Je ne sais pas. Celle qui est jolie.

– .... ?
– La bleue.

– Et .... chaussures veux-tu porter ?
– Celles qui sont confortables.

– Mais .... ?
– Les sandales.

– Et .... chapeau aimerais-tu ?
– Celui avec une fleur. Merci ! »

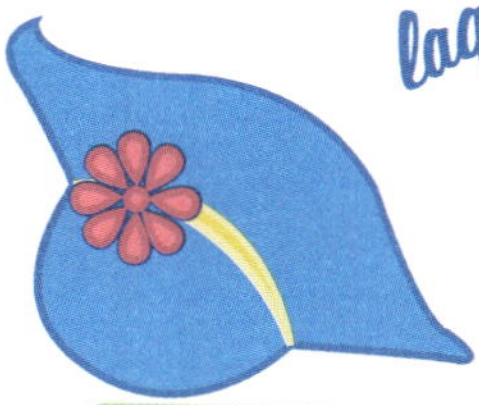

Possessive pronouns

- French possessive pronouns have four forms: masculine singular, feminine singular, masculine plural and feminine plural.
- A possessive pronoun takes the place of a possessive adjective + noun: **ma montre** *my watch* → **la mienne** *mine* (f. sing.). A possessive pronoun must agree in gender and number with what is possessed, not the possessor.
- The French possessive pronouns are shown in the table:

ENGLISH	FRENCH
mine	le mien, la mienne les miens, les miennes
yours (sing. informal)	le tien, la tienne les tiens, les tiennes
his/hers	le sien, la sienne, les siens, les siennes
ours	le nôtre, la nôtre les nôtres
yours (plural/ formal)	le vôtre, la vôtre, les vôtres
theirs	le leur, la leur les leurs

7 Choose the appropriate possessive pronoun as shown in the example below.

E.g. J'aime mon beau blouson ! → J'aime le mien.

a. J'aime leur belle voiture. → J'aime ....

b. J'aime son beau sac à main. → J'aime ....

c. J'aime nos beaux chaussons. → J'aime ....

d. J'aime ta jolie robe. → J'aime ....

e. J'aime ses superbes chaussures. → J'aime ....

Relative pronouns

A relative pronoun is used to link a relative clause with a noun that has previously been mentioned in order to give more information about it.

- **qui** and **que** can mean *which* or *that* referring to objects: *I have a new car that goes very fast!* → **J'ai une nouvelle voiture qui va très vite !** – *The book that I read is great!* → **Le livre que j'ai lu est génial !**
- **qui** is used to refer to people, i.e. *who*: **L'homme qui était dans la rue.** *The man who was in the street.*
- **que** is used before a noun (**Le film que Raphaël regarde.**) and **qui** before a verb (**Le film qui a gagné le prix.**).
- To refer to a clause rather than a sole noun, use **ce que** or **ce qui**: *She never stops talking, which I find really annoying.* → **Elle ne s'arrête jamais de parler, ce que je trouve très énervant.**

8 *QUI* or *QUE*? Circle the correct relative pronoun in these sentences.

a. L'enfant **que / qui** pleurait était perdu.

b. Le dernier film **que / qui** j'ai vu était merveilleux.

c. La tarte **que / qui** maman a préparée est délicieuse !

d. Je connais la femme **que / qui** est devant la boutique.

e. Je déteste le parfum **que / qui** tu portes aujourd'hui.

9 *CE QUE* or *CE QUI* ? Circle the correct form in the following sentences.

a. Le bébé a pleuré toute la nuit, **ce que / ce qui** j'ai trouvé fatigant.
b. Il pleut encore, **ce que / ce qui** est très ennuyeux.
c. Je t'ai dit de ranger ta chambre, **ce que / ce qui** je t'ai déjà demandé 3 fois !
d. Le professeur est absent, **ce que / ce qui** signifie que nous pouvons rentrer chez nous.
e. Il a amené des fleurs, **ce que / ce qui** je trouve très gentil.

En / y

- The French pronoun **en** means *of it* or *of them*. This pronoun comes before the verb: **Combien de films a-t-il ? Il en a 15.** → *How many films does he have? He has 15 (of them).*
- The pronoun **y** means *here, there*. It also comes before the verb: *She is going to France next year; she is going there by plane.* → **Elle va en France l'année prochaine; elle y va en avion.**
- Note: in the negative, **ne** becomes **n'** in front of **en** and **y**: **Je n'en ai pas.** *I don't have any.* **Je n'y vais pas.** *I'm not going there.*

10 Complete the sentences with either *en* or *y* given the context.

a. As-tu des livres ?
Oui j'.............. ai.

b. Est-il passé au bureau ?
Oui, il .... est allé.

c. As-tu acheté des poires ?
Non, je n'.................... ai pas acheté.

d. Avons-nous des stylos noirs ?
Oui, nous .... avons.

e. Jacques était-il au magasin ?
Non, il n'.................... était pas.

Chouette ! You have completed Lesson 7! Count up the icons for the exercises and record your result here and in the table on page 128.

8
Numbers and time

Numbers

Let's look at the numbers in French.

- The good news is that there is only one number (**un**, *one*) that has two forms for gender: **un lapin** *(one rabbit)* but **une tortue** *(one turtle)*.
- When they come after a number and are not followed by another number, **vingt** *twenty* and **cent** *hundred* take an **-s**:
  quatre-vingt-douze → quatre-vingts
  deux cent cinquante → deux cents
- **mille** *thousand* never takes an **s**.

1 Do you know the numbers in French? Fill in the blanks.

1	*un/une*	**19**	*dix-neuf*	80	
2	*deux*	**20**	*vingt*	**81**	*quatre-vingt-un*
3	*trois*	21		**82**	*quatre-vingt-deux*
4	*quatre*	**22**	*vingt-deux*	90	
5	*cinq*	**30**	*trente*	**91**	*quatre-vingt-onze*
6	*six*	**31**	*trente et un*	**92**	*quatre-vingt-douze*
7	*sept*	**32**	*trente-deux*		
8		**40**	*quarante*		
9	*neuf*	**41**	*quarante et un*		
10	*dix*	**42**	*quarante-deux*		
11	*onze*	50			
12	*douze*	70			
13	*treize*	**74**	*soixante-quatorze*		
14		**75**	*soixante-quinze*		
15	*quinze*	76			
16	*seize*	**77**	*soixante-dix-sept*		
17	*dix-sept*	**78**	*soixante-dix-huit*		
18	*dix-huit*	**79**	*soixante-dix-neuf*		

100	*cent*
101	*cent un*
102	*cent deux*
200	
201	*deux cent un*
202	*deux cent deux*
1 000	*mille*
2 000	
2 001	*deux mille un*
2 002	*deux mille deux*
100 000	*cent mille*
1 000 000	*un million*

2 Match each calculation to the correct answer.

2 + 5	=	quatre-vingts
10 x 8	=	vingt et un
9 x 2	=	soixante-treize
10 000 ÷ 10	=	sept
51 + 22	=	soixante-quatorze
30 – 9	=	mille
35 + 39	=	trente-six
216 ÷ 6	=	dix-huit

3 Write these numbers in figures. One figure has a mathematical difference from the others: which one is it?

douze

cinquante-deux

cent quarante-six

cinq cent quatre-vingt-huit

onze

mille huit cents

six

Ordinal numbers

When used as adjectives, ordinal numbers in French (*first*, *second*, *third*, etc.) must agree in gender and number with a noun: **le premier livre, la première fille, les premiers livres, les premières filles.**

4 Complete the table with the ordinal numbers in French.

1er	*premier*	12^{e}	*douzième*	23^{e}	*vingt-troisième*
2^{e}	*deuxième*	13^{e}	*treizième*	24^{e}	*vingt-quatrième*
3^{e}	*troisième*	14^{e}	*quatorzième*	25^{e}	*vingt-cinquième*
4^{e}		15^{e}	*quinzième*	26^{e}	
5^{e}	*cinquième*	16^{e}		27^{e}	*vingt-septième*
6^{e}	*sixième*	17^{e}		28^{e}	*vingt-huitième*
7^{e}	*septième*	18^{e}	*dix-huitième*	29^{e}	*vingt-neuvième*
8^{e}	*huitième*	19^{e}	*dix-neuvième*	30^{e}	*trentième*
9^{e}		20^{e}	*vingtième*	40^{e}	*quarantième*
10^{e}	*dixième*	21^{e}		70^{e}	*soixante-dixième*
11^{e}	*onzième*	22^{e}	*vingt-deuxième*		

100^{e}	*centième*
$1\ 000^{e}$	

5 Put the letters in order to find the ordinal numbers.

a. ÈAURIAMEQTN = __________

b. TNGUMENNEÈTCVIVIE = ____ ______________

c. RREEIMP = _______

d. ÈONIEMXISAT = ___________

e. MMELIÈIL = ________

f. RITTEÈEMN = _________

Days and months

The names of days and months are masculine in French and are not capitalized: **lundi 4 janvier** *Monday, 4 January.*

6 Complete the missing days of the week.

lundi

....

mercredi

....

vendredi

....

....

7 Complete the missing months of the year.

janvier

....

mars

....

mai

....

juillet

....

septembre

....

novembre

....

8 Translate the following sentences into English.

a. J'ai vu Jean-Philippe avant-hier.

= ....

b. Qu'as-tu fait le lendemain ?

= ....

c. Veux-tu aller au cinéma vendredi prochain ?

= ....

d. Ella a vu ce film mardi dernier.

= ....

e. Il fait vraiment beau aujourd'hui !

= ....

Some useful words and phrases

on Monday **lundi**

on Mondays, every Monday **le lundi**

yesterday **hier**

today **aujourd'hui**

tomorrow **demain**

last Tuesday **mardi dernier**

next Thursday **jeudi prochain**

the day before **la veille**

the day after **le lendemain**

the day after tomorrow **après-demain**

the day before yesterday **avant-hier**

What time is it? (*Quelle heure est-il ?*)

Il est … *It is …*

midi *midday, noon*

minuit *midnight*

deux heures *two o'clock*

trois heures et quart *a quarter past three*

quatre heures et demie *half past four*

cinq heures moins le quart *a quarter to five*

six heures dix *ten past six*

sept heures moins vingt *twenty to seven*

à l'heure *on time*

à temps *in time*

un quart d'heure *a quarter of an hour*

une demie-heure *a half hour*

à sept heures du matin *at seven in the morning*

à trois heures de l'après-midi *at three in the afternoon*

à sept heures du soir *at seven in the evening*

9 Write out the times in words next to each clock.

a. Quelle heure est-il ?
Il est (13h15)

....

b. Quelle heure est-il ?
Il est (16h30)

....

c. Quelle heure est-il ?
Il est (4h45)

....

d. Quelle heure est-il ?
Il est (20h40)

....

e. Quelle heure est-il ?
Il est (10h25)

....

10 Use Mr Dupouy's diary to fill in his schedule for each day (at the top of the next page) with the times written in words.

Lundi 3 mai	Mardi 4 mai	Mercredi 5 mai
9h00 : *Réunion au bureau*	9h30 : *Rendez-vous Dr Garrant*	8h20 : *Petit déjeuner d'affaires*
	11h00 : *Réunion à La Défense*	
12h30 : *Déjeuner avec M. Gosseaume*	12h20 : *Déjeuner avec Bastian à Montmartre*	13h45 : *Conférence à Dijon*
14h10 : *Présentation nouveau produit*	14h15 : *Aéroport Retour Dijon*	
18h25 : *Aéroport départ pour Paris*	19h00 : *Dîner avec Marie*	18h00 : *Réunion parents d'élèves*

Lundi à ______________ M. Dupouy doit se rendre à une réunion qui a lieu au bureau. À ______________, il déjeune avec M. Gosseaume à la Brasserie Dijonnaise puis à ______________, il participe à la présentation du nouveau produit de la compagnie. Le soir même, à ______________, il prend l'avion pour Paris.

Le lendemain, M. Dupouy a un rendez-vous avec Dr Garrant à ______________, suivi d'une réunion à La Défense à ______________. Il doit déjeuner à Montmartre à ______________ avec son ami Bastian puis se rend à l'aéroport pour son vol de ______________. Il dîne avec sa femme, Marie à ______________.

Le mercredi, M. Dupouy a un déjeuner avec un collaborateur à ______________ puis doit se rendre à une conférence à ______________ à Dijon. À ______________, il doit aller à l'école de son fils pour rencontrer l'instituteur.

II Find the answers to the following problems.

a. Lundi, Louis dépense la moitié de son argent ; mardi, il dépense le tiers de ce qu'il reste ; mercredi, il a 30 €. Combien avait Louis lundi ?

....

b. Dans sa tirelire, Élise a des pièces de 50 cents et de 10 cents. En tout, elle a 4 €. Combien a-t-elle de pièces de 50 cents sachant qu'il y a 10 pièces de 10 cents ?

....

c. Un fermier a des poules et des lapins. En examinant tous les animaux, il voit 5 têtes et 16 pattes. Combien y a-t-il de lapins et de poules ?

....

d. Marc cuisine 8 tartelettes en 40 minutes. Combien de temps lui faut-il pour préparer 160 tartelettes ?

....

Good work! You have completed Lesson 8! It's time to count up the icons for the exercises and record your result here and in the table on page 128.

9

Verbs & the perfect tense

The infinitive (*L'infinitif*)

- An infinitive is the basic, unconjugated form of a verb, e.g. *to say*. French verbs are divided into three categories, depending on the infinitive ending:
  - 1st group: **-er** (e.g. **aimer** *to love*)
  - 2nd group: **-ir** (e.g. **finir** *to finish*)
  - 3rd group: **-re**, **-ir**, **-oir**, etc. (**vendre** *to sell*, **dormir** *to sleep*, **voir** *to see*)

Each group conjugates in a slightly different way. That is, the (regular) verbs in a group take the same endings in the different tenses. The 3rd group is irregular.

- To make an infinitive negative, **ne pas** is placed in front of it: **ne pas manger** *not to eat*.
- In French, when two verbs are used together, the second verb must always be an infinitive: **Je dois aller au bureau**.

1 Write the infinitive of the underlined verbs.

a. J'ai mangé trop de gâteaux !

→ ....

b. Ils ont bu toute la limonade !

→ ....

c. Où vas-tu ce matin ?

→ ....

d. Je dormirai dans le salon.

→ ....

e. Je voudrais bien gagner au loto !

→ ....

2 First, second or third group? Tick the right column.

	1st group	2nd group	3rd group
chanter	☐	☐	☐
punir	☐	☐	☐
rendre	☐	☐	☐
écouter	☐	☐	☐
pleuvoir	☐	☐	☐
grandir	☐	☐	☐
devenir	☐	☐	☐
danser	☐	☐	☐
apprendre	☐	☐	☐

Past participles (*Le participe passé*)

- The past participle (the form of a verb typically ending in *-ed* in English, e.g. *looked*) is formed by replacing the infinitive ending with the past participle ending, according to the verb group. (However, some very frequent verbs such as **aller** or **faire** are irregular.)

- A past participle can be used as a verb (**j'ai fini** / *have finished*) or an adjective (**je suis fatigué** / *am tired*).

Forming a past participle (regular verbs)

	Infinitive	Ending	Drop	Add	Past participle
1st group	**donner**	-er	-er	-é	donné
2nd group	**finir**	-ir	-ir	-i	fini
3rd group	**vendre**	-re	-re	-u	vendu

3 Complete the following table.

	INFINITIVE	PAST PARTICIPLE
Nous étudions le français.	étudier	étudié
a. Il déteste les chats !	....	....
b. Nous dînons généralement tôt.	....	....
c. Elle aime beaucoup le théâtre.	....	....
d. J'écoute mon CD préféré.	....	....
e. Sophie perd régulièrement ses clés !	....	....
f. Prends-tu le train tous les matins ?	....	....

4 Write the past participle of these irregular verbs.

a. Hier, nous avons .... **(apprendre)** une nouvelle leçon !

b. Il m'a .... **(offrir)** un magnifique bouquet de roses !

c. Elle a .... **(vouloir)** rentrer tôt à la maison.

d. Nous avons .... **(pouvoir)** rencontrer le chanteur du groupe.

e. Vous avez .... **(faire)** vos devoirs ?

Past participle agreement

- When a past participle is used in the perfect tense with the auxiliary verb **avoir** (e.g. **j'ai donné** *I have given*), it only agrees with the direct object when the object comes before the verb: **J'ai envoyé la lettre hier. – Je l'ai envoyée hier.**
- There is no agreement when the direct object comes after the verb.
- But a past participle with the auxiliary verb **être** must agree with the subject in gender and number: **Elle est allée au théâtre. – Elles sont allées au théâtre.**

5 Complete each sentence with the past participle of these verbs that use *avoir* in the perfect tense.

a. Elles ont .... **(lire)** tous les livres.

b. Elles les ont tous .... **(lire)**.

c. Nous avons .... **(copier)** toutes les pages.

d. Nous les avons toutes .... **(copier)**.

e. Elle n'a pas .... **(pleurer)** longtemps.

6 **Complete each sentence with the past participle of these verbs that use *être* in the perfect tense.**

a. Elle est .... **(aller)** en ville avec Sonia.

b. Clarèle et moi *(m.)* sommes .... **(rentrer)** à midi.

c. Éléanore et Audrey sont .... **(partir)** après le film.

d. Alain n'est pas .... **(arriver)**.

e. Jean-Luc et Jérôme sont .... **(venir)** à 18 heures.

Reflexive verbs in perfect tenses

- Reflexive verbs (e.g. **se laver** *to wash oneself*) conjugate in the perfect tense with the auxiliary verb **être**.
- If the reflexive pronoun is a direct object, the past participle agrees; if it is an indirect object, it does not:

Elle	**s'**	**est**	**lavée.**
subject	*direct object*	*aux. verb*	*past participle*
Elle	**s'**	**est**	**lavé les mains.**
subject	*indirect object*	*aux. verb*	*past part. + direct object*

7 **Complete the sentences with the correct verb.**

a. Ils se sont encore .... !

b. Elles se sont .... leurs adresses.

c. Elle s'est .... le doigt.

d. Elles se sont .... devant la télé.

e. Ils se sont .... pendant de longues minutes.

coupé

regardés

disputés

échangé

endormies

The perfect tense (*Le passé composé*)

- In French, the present perfect is used to describe an action or event that occurred in the past and is completely finished. It often translates to the simple past in English: **il est allé** *he went* or *he has gone*. For example, it is used to talk about the weather at a specific time in the past: **Il a plu vendredi.**
- It is formed with either **avoir** or **être** conjugated in the present + past participle of the main verb.

Verbs that take *être* in the perfect tense

- Although most verbs form the perfect tense with **avoir**, certain verbs use **être** as the auxiliary verb.
- When the perfect tense is formed with **être**, the past participle must agree with the subject of the verb.
- The verbs that take **être** as an auxiliary in the perfect tense are verbs related to movement or a change of state. There are a limited number of these so they aren't too hard to remember!

aller (allé) - **arriver** (arrivé) - **descendre** (descendu) - **entrer** (entré) - **monter** (monté) - **mourir** (mort) - **naître** (né) - **partir** (parti) - **rentrer** (rentré) - **rester** (resté) - **retourner** (retourné) - **sortir** (sorti) - **tomber** (tombé) - **venir** (venu)

8 Connect each subject to the rest of the sentence.

1. J'	a. avons vu ta sœur ce matin.
2. Nous	b. ont rangé leur chambre.
3. Tu	c. ai gagné la course !
4. Elles	d. êtes restés au parc toute la journée ?
5. Vous	e. es rentrée à quelle heure ?
6. Ils	f. sont allées au marché ce matin.

9 Underline the correct form of the past participle.

a. Nous avons **regardé / regardés / regardées** la télévision toute la nuit !

b. Elles sont **entré / entrés / entrées** par la porte de secours.

c. J'ai **mis / mise / mises** la voiture dans le garage.

d. Tu as **vu / vus / vues** l'éclipse hier soir ?

e. Samuel et Laurence ont **écouté / écoutés / écoutées** la radio pendant deux heures !

f. Nous avons **pris / prise / prises** un taxi pour rentrer.

10 Rewrite the sentences, conjugating the infinitives in the perfect tense (with *elles*), and list them in chronological order.

a. rester deux heures au restaurant.

b. arriver à la gare à six heures.

c. rentrer à l'hôtel se coucher.

d. déposer leurs bagages dans la chambre.

e. téléphoner à l'hôtel pour réserver une chambre.

f. demander au concierge l'adresse d'un bon restaurant.

1. Elles sont arrivées à la gare à six heures.

2. ....

3. ....

4. ....

5. ....

6. ....

C'est ça ! You've finished Lesson 9! It's time to count up the icons for the exercises and record your results here and in the table on page 128.

10

Talking about the present

The present tense (*Le présent*)

- As in English, the present tense is used to talk about something taking place now, something that habitually occurs, or something that will occur soon. The French present tense can also translate to the English present continuous: **je mange** *I eat* or *I am eating*.
- The present tense is formed differently for the three verb groups:
  - 1st group (infinitive ending in **-er**): the conjugations are shown in the table on the right.
  - 2nd group (ending in **-ir**): the infinitive ending is replaced with **-is, -is, -it, -issons, -issez, -issent**
  - 3rd group (ending in **-re, -ir** or **-oir**, etc.): these are irregular verbs so the endings vary.

Regular verbs ending in *-er*

j'	aime
tu	aimes
il/elle	aime
nous	aimons
vous	aimez
ils/elles	aiment

1 Underline the correct subject pronoun.

a. **Je / Tu / Nous** marches vite.

b. **Tu / Nous / Elles** chantent sous la pluie.

c. **Je / Tu / Vous** porte des chaussures.

d. **Elle / Nous / Ils** aidons les sans-abris.

e. **Tu / Nous / Vous** dansez très bien !

f. **Je / Tu / Elles** pense trop !

2 Underline the correct form of the verb.

a. Les touristes **visites / visitent** le musée.

b. Tu **portes / portons** une jolie jupe.

c. Nous **aimons / aiment** la musique classique.

d. À quelle heure **arrive / arrivez** -vous ?

e. Il **chante / chantes** très bien.

3 Conjugate the following verbs in the present tense.

a. Je .... **(travailler)** dans l'informatique.

b. Tu .... **(visiter)** ce musée souvent ?

c. Il .... **(débuter)** le travail à 10 heures.

d. Nous .... **(dessiner)** ce château régulièrement.

e. Vous ne .... **(monter)** pas les escaliers ?

f. Elles .... **(parler)** trop vite !

Irregular *-er* verbs

There is only one real irregular **-er** verb: **aller** *to go*. However, certain verbs have spelling changes in the stem in certain persons in the present tense.

- Verbs ending in **-cer** replace the **c** with a **ç** in the first-person plural (**nous**): **Nous remplaçons les ampoules.**
- Verbs ending in **-ger** add an **-e** in the first-person plural (**nous**): **Nous rangeons notre chambre.**

- In the following **-er** verbs, the spelling change indicated occurs in all persons except for the first- and second-person plural (**nous** and **vous**):

– Verbs like **acheter**: **e > è = j'achète**
– Verbs like **appeler**: **l > ll = elle appelle**
– Verbs like **envoyer**: **y > i = j'envoie**
– Verbs like **espérer**: **é > è = il espère**
– Verbs like **nettoyer**: **y > i = tu nettoies**

4 Underline the correct spelling of the verb.

a. Nous **achètons / achetons** des pizzas tous les samedis.

b. Qui **appellent / appelent** -ils ?

c. Il **jette / jète** ses vieilles chaussures.

d. Vous **espérez / espèrez** encore voir Brad Pitt !

e. Nous **envoieons / envoyons** la lettre.

5 Conjugate these verbs with spelling changes following the rules above.

a. Nous ....
(commencer) la réunion à 10 heures.

b. Je ....
(préférer) le pain complet.

c. Nous ....
(manger) au restaurant ce midi.

d. Tu te ....
(rappeler) le dernier livre que tu as lu ?

e. Elle lui ....
(envoyer) une lettre chaque semaine.

Present tense of *-ir* verbs

je	finis
tu	finis
il/elle	finit
nous	finissons
vous	finissez
ils/elles	finissent

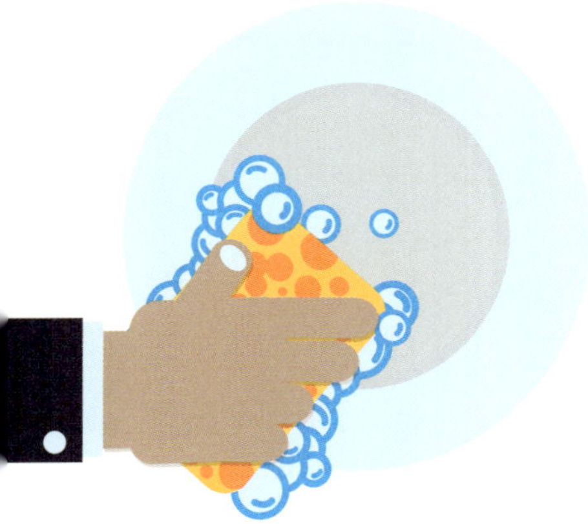

6 Conjugate the verbs in these sentences in the present tense.

a. Tu .... (choisir) d'étudier l'anglais ?

b. Nous .... (réussir) toujours les examens d'histoire.

c. Elle .... (maigrir) à vue d'œil !

d. Jacques .... (punir) souvent son fils.

e. Vous ne .... (réfléchir) pas assez !

7 Underline the right form of the verb.

a. Je **choisi / choisis** toujours la mauvaise caisse au supermarché !

b. Nous **finons / finissons** souvent avant le reste de la classe.

c. Vous **bâtez / bâtissez** une nouvelle maison ?

d. Ils **réussent / réussissent** toujours à éviter de faire la vaisselle !

e. Tu **remplis / remplit** trop mon verre !

Present tense of regular *-re* verbs

je	vends
tu	vends
il/elle	vend
nous	vendons
vous	vendez
ils/elles	vendent

8 Conjugate these regular *-re* verbs.

a. Tu .... (descendre) au prochain arrêt ?

b. Vous .... (perdre) toujours de l'argent au casino !

c. Sophie et Marc .... (vendre) de très jolies fleurs dans leur magasin.

d. Nous .... (défendre) souvent notre sœur.

e. Ils n'.................. (entendre) pas la cloche de l'église !

Irregular verbs

- There are a number of irregular verbs that don't follow the regular patterns in every person. Here are five **-re** verbs with irregularities in the present tense:

prendre *to take*: je prends, tu prends, il/elle prend, nous prenons, vous prenez, ils/elles prennent (no **d** in all plural forms and double **n** in the 3rd-person plural)

battre *to beat*: je bats, tu bats, il/elle bat, nous battons, vous battez, ils/elles battent (drop one **t** in the singular forms)

mettre *to put*: je mets, tu mets, il/elle met, nous mettons, vous mettez, ils/elles mettent (like *battre* in the present tense, but also irregular in certain other tenses)

rompre *to break*: je romps, tu romps, il/elle rompt, nous rompons, vous rompez, ils/elles rompent (3rd-person singular adds a **-t**)

- Verbs in **-aindre** (**craindre** *to fear / to be afraid of*) and **-eindre** (**peindre** *to paint*) conjugate as follows: je crains, tu crains, il/elle craint, nous craignons, vous craignez, ils/elles craignent (no **-d** in all forms, 3rd-person singular adds a **-t**, and a **-g** is added before the **-n** in all plural forms).

- Here is the present tense of some other common irregular verbs:

aller *to go*: je vais, tu vas, il/elle va, nous allons, vous allez, ils/elles vont

boire *to drink*: je bois, tu bois, il/elle boit, nous buvons, vous buvez, ils/elles boivent

connaître *to know (someone or a place)*: je connais, tu connais, il/elle connaît, nous connaissons, vous connaissez, ils/elles connaissent

courir *to run*: je cours, tu cours, il/elle court, nous courons, vous courez, ils/elles courent

croire *to believe*: je crois, tu crois, il/elle croit, nous croyons, vous croyez, ils/elles croient

devoir *to have to*: je dois, tu dois, il/elle doit, nous devons, vous devez, ils/elles doivent

dire *to say*: je dis, tu dis, il/elle dit, nous disons, vous dites, ils/elles disent

faire *to do*: je fais, tu fais, il/elle fait, nous faisons, vous faites, ils/elles font

falloir *to be necessary*: il faut

lire *to read*: je lis, tu lis, il/elle lit, nous lisons, vous lisez, ils/elles lisent

pouvoir *to be able to*: je peux, tu peux, il/elle peut, nous pouvons, vous pouvez, ils/elles peuvent

savoir *to know (how)*: je sais, tu sais, il/elle sait, nous savons, vous savez, ils/elles savent

tenir *to hold*: je tiens, tu tiens, il/elle tient, nous tenons, vous tenez, ils/elles tiennent

venir *to come*: je viens, tu viens, il/elle vient, nous venons, vous venez, ils/elles viennent

voir *to see*: je vois, tu vois, il/elle voit, nous voyons, vous voyez, ils/elles voient

vouloir *to want*: je veux, tu veux, il/elle veut, nous voulons, vous voulez, ils/elles veulent

9 Complete the sentences with the correct verb.

a. Où ....-tu les sacs de voyage ?

b. .... -vous à quelle heure part le train ?

c. Nous .... voyager en avion cette fois-ci.

d. ....-tu porter cette valise, s'il te plaît ?

e. Nous .... aller au terminal 1 ou au terminal 2 ?

f. Je ne .... pas notre porte de départ !

Reflexive verbs (*Les verbes pronominaux*)

- When conjugating a reflexive verb, the pronoun needs to change.
- In front of a vowel or a silent **h**, **me, te** and **se** become **m', t'** and **s'**.

10 Underline the correct reflexive pronoun in each case (it should mirror the subject pronoun).

a. Je **me / te / se** douche tous les matins.

b. Elle **me / te / se** brosse les dents deux fois par jour.

c. Nous **nous / vous / se** lavons les mains constamment !

d. Vous **nous / vous / se** rongez encore les ongles !

e. Ils **nous / vous / s'** habillent à 7h15 tous les jours.

The imperative (*L'impératif*)

- The imperative is the verb form used to give a command, make a request, give advice or encourage someone to do something. It is the same as the present tense (just use the appropriate person without a subject pronoun).
- The imperative is used in three persons: **tu**, **nous** and **vous** (formal or plural).

tu form	**Prends le parapluie.**	*Take the umbrella.*
nous form	**Prenons le parapluie.**	*Let's take the umbrella.*
vous form	**Prenez le parapluie.**	*Take the umbrella.*

- In **-er** verbs, the final **-s** in the second-person singular (**tu** form) is dropped: **Chante ! / Ne chante pas !**
- A few verbs use the present subjunctive to form the imperative.

avoir	être	vouloir
aie	sois	--
ayons	soyons	--
ayez	soyez	veuillez

11 **Conjugate these verbs in the imperative form indicated.**
E.g. (écrire/tu) sur le cahier. → Écris sur le cahier.

a. .... **(écouter/tu)** le professeur !

b. Ne .... **(regarder/vous)** pas par la fenêtre, mais .... **(lire/vous)** votre livre !

c. .... **(arrêter/tu)** de parler avec ton voisin !

d. .... **(rendre/nous)** nos copies. Le test est terminé.

e. .... **(prendre/vous)** vos livres et .... **(ouvrir)**-les à la page 47.

The imperative with object pronouns

In affirmative commands, an object pronoun comes after the verb and is linked to it with a hyphen:

Range-les ! *Put them away!*

Vendez-la ! *Sell it!*

12 **Put the verb in the imperative and add the appropriate pronoun.**
E.g. Tu vois le titre? (souligner) → Souligne-le.

a. Tu vois le poème ? .... (apprendre).

b. Vous voyez les livres ? .... (ranger).

c. Tu vois la raquette de tennis ? .... (prendre).

d. Nous voyons les ordinateurs. .... (éteindre).

e. Vous voyez le poster ? .... (accrocher).

Bravo ! You've reached the end of Lesson 10. It's time to count up the icons for the exercises and record your result here and in the table on page 128.

11

Talking about the future

The future tense (*Le futur*)

- As in English, the future tense is used to talk about an action or a state that will occur at a point in time in the future.
- Some good news! All verbs take the same endings in the future tense. These endings are simply added to the infinitive of **-er** and **-ir** verbs; **-re** verbs first drop the **-e** from the infinitive and then add the endings.

	aimer	**finir**	**vendre**
je/j'	**aimerai**	**finirai**	**vendrai**
tu	**aimeras**	**finiras**	**vendras**
il/elle	**aimera**	**finira**	**vendra**
nous	**aimerons**	**finirons**	**vendrons**
vous	**aimerez**	**finirez**	**vendrez**
ils/elles	**aimeront**	**finiront**	**vendront**

1 Complete the sentences with the appropriate verb in the future tense.

a. Demain, quand le réveil sonnera, je .... mon maillot de bain.

b. Nous .... au restaurant pour prendre notre petit déjeuner.

c. Comme tous les matins, le serveur nous .... notre cappuccino.

d. Tu .... une salade de fruits frais.

e. Nous nous .... dans l'océan turquoise.

baignerons · *servira* · *descendrons* · *mettrai* · *mangeras*

2 Conjugate the following verbs in the future tense.

a. Nous .... **(danser)** toute la nuit !

b. Vous ..... **(choisir)** quoi comme vin, messieurs-dames ?

c. .... **(prendre)**-tu de l'eau ?

d. Elles .... **(chanter)** longtemps à la soirée karaoké.

e. Il .... **(rentrer)** tard, c'est sûr !

Irregular verbs in the future

Certain verbs do not use the infinitive as the stem for the future tense. Here is a list of some of the most common:

aller *to go*: j'irai, tu iras, il/elle ira, nous irons, vous irez, ils/elles iront

avoir *to have*: j'aurai, tu auras, il/elle aura, nous aurons, vous aurez, ils/elles auront

courir *to run*: je courrai, tu courras, il/elle courra, nous courrons, vous courrez, ils/elles courront

devoir *to have to*: je devrai, tu devras, il/elle devra, nous devrons, vous devrez, ils/elles devront

envoyer *to send*: j'enverrai, tu enverras, il/elle enverra, nous enverrons, vous enverrez, ils/elles enverront

être *to be*: je serai, tu seras, il/elle sera, nous serons, vous serez, ils/elles seront

faire *to do*: je ferai, tu feras, il/elle fera, nous ferons, vous ferez, ils/elles feront

mourir *to die*: je mourrai, tu mourras, il/elle mourra, nous mourrons, vous mourrez, ils/elles mourront

pouvoir *to be able to*: je pourrai, tu pourras, il/elle pourra, nous pourrons, vous pourrez, ils/elles pourront

savoir *to know*: je saurai, tu sauras, il/elle saura, nous saurons, vous saurez, ils/elles sauront

tenir *to hold*: je tiendrai, tu tiendras, il/elle tiendra, nous tiendrons, vous tiendrez, ils/elles tiendront

venir *to come*: je viendrai, tu viendras, il/elle viendra, nous viendrons, vous viendrez, ils/elles viendront

voir *to see*: je verrai, tu verras, il/elle verra, nous verrons, vous verrez, ils/elles verront

vouloir *to want*: je voudrai, tu voudras, il/elle voudra, nous voudrons, vous voudrez, ils/elles voudront

3 Use the list of irregular verbs on the previous page to help you select the correct future tense form.

1. Ta lettre est géniale. L'..................-tu à Stéphanie ?

a. ☐ envoya **b.** ☐ enverra **c.** ☐ enverras

2. On s'est bien amusées aujourd'hui ! Que ....-nous demain ?

a. ☐ faisions **b.** ☐ ferons **c.** ☐ ferrons

3. Cet hôtel est fantastique ! ....-vous à nouveau l'année prochaine ?

a. ☐ Viendrez **b.** ☐ Viendriez **c.** ☐ Veniez

4. Le trajet est facile. ....-vous retrouver la route ?

a. ☐ saurai **b.** ☐ saurez **c.** ☐ sauriez

5. Quelle journée bien remplie ! Où ....-nous après le restaurant ?

a. ☐ allions **b.** ☐ allons **c.** ☐ irons

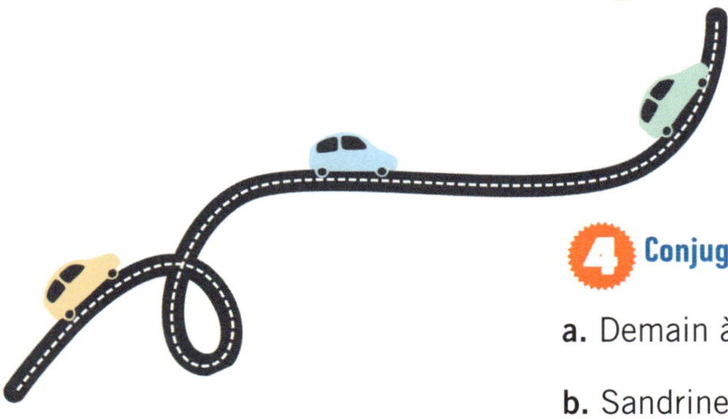

4 Conjugate these verbs in the future tense.

a. Demain à la même heure, je .... **(être)** à la plage !

b. Sandrine, ... **(avoir)**-tu ton téléphone portable avec toi au restaurant ?

c. Vous .... **(voir)** ! La piscine de l'hôtel est formidable !

d. .... **(pouvoir)**-nous faire garder notre petite fille ?

e. Nos filles .... **(aller)** en excursion la semaine prochaine !

5 **Underline the 10 verbs conjugated in the future tense in the following text.**

« Marie est très heureuse. Demain, Charles arrivera par le train, un bouquet à la main, prêt à l'épouser. Ils se regarderont et à cet instant précis, se reconnaîtront, pour la vie. Pour le meilleur, et pour le pire. Ils voyageront autour du monde, visiteront tous ces pays dont ils ont parlé sans se lasser. Ils pourront parler sans interruption. Qui sait ? Ils se marieront ; auront des enfants, peut-être. Et vivront dans la paix, sans cette guerre qui a ravagé leur pays. Enfin. Le bonheur. Qui pourrait les en empêcher ? Ils seront ensemble, unis, contre tous. »

The near future

- In French, the present tense is often used to talk about an event in the near future: **Demain, je mange au restaurant.** *I am going out to eat tomorrow.*

- **aller** (in the present tense) + infinitive
Another way to talk about the future is to use the verb **aller** *to go* in the present tense followed by an infinitive, indicating that something is going to happen: **Je vais partir en vacances demain.** *I am going on holiday tomorrow.* **Il va observer les étoiles ce soir.** *He is going to stargaze tonight.*

6 **Conjugate *aller* in the present tense for each person.**

a. je ....
b. tu ....
c. il/elle ....
d. nous ....
e. vous ....
f. ils/elles ....

7 Underline the correct near future form of *aller* (present tense) + infinitive.

a. Nous allions / allons / irons voir le nouveau film de Jean Dujardin demain !

b. Allez / Alliez / Irez-vous assister au spectacle ?

c. Je ne allez / irai / vais pas manger chez Chloé demain midi.

d. Il va / allait / irait encore manger du chocolat en cachette !

e. Quand vas / iras / allé -tu aller poster les cartes de Noël ?

8 Put these verbs in the near future using *aller* (present tense) + infinitive.

a. Dépêchez-vous ! Le spectacle .... (aller + commencer) !

b. Ta voiture est en panne ? Pas de problème ! Je .... te .... (aller + conduire) au garage.

c. Le ciel se couvre : je pense qu'il .... (aller + pleuvoir).

d. Les Lagrange .... (aller + visiter) le Vietnam au mois d'août.

e. ....-vous .... (aller + partir) en vacances cette année ?

The near future in the negative

- **ne**...**pas** negates **aller** (not the other verb): **Elle ne va pas venir au cinéma ce soir.**
- The same rule applies with a reflexive verb: **Il ne va pas se lever à huit heures demain matin.**

9 Make the following statements negative.

a. Je vais suivre des cours à l'université.

➜ ....

b. Julie va passer son permis de conduire la semaine prochaine.

➜ ....

c. Elles vont se promener en ville cet après-midi.

➜ ....

d. Allez-vous rentrer à dix heures ce soir ?

➜ .... ?

e. Tu vas rester à la maison demain ?

➜ .... ?

The future tense after specific terms

The future tense must be used after certain terms: **aussitôt que** / **dès que** *as soon as*, **quand** / **lorsque** *when*, **tant que** *as long as*, **pendant que** / **tandis que** *while*: **Je dormirai lorsqu'il arrivera.** *I will sleep when he gets* ('will get') *here*.

10 Conjugate the following verbs in the future tense.

a. Je .... **(partir)** quand Alexandre .... **(arriver)**.

b. Dorian .... **(aller)** chez son frère demain après-midi.

c. Élise .... **(être)** déçue lorsqu'elle .... **(apprendre)** que Corentin ne vient pas.

d. Nous .... **(venir)** tous en vacances avec vous l'année prochaine ! Plus on est de fous, plus on rit !

e. Que .... **(faire)**-tu demain à cette heure-ci ?

Great! You've completed Lesson 11! It's time to count up the icons for the exercises and record your result here and in the table on page 128.

12 The past and the conditional

The imperfect tense (*L'imparfait*)

- The imperfect tense is used to talk about things that used to happen regularly in the past: **Quand j'étais petite, j'allais chez mon grand-père tous les mercredis.** *When I was little, I used to go to my grandfather's every Wednesday.*
- It is also used to describe what something was like in the past: **Il y avait beaucoup de monde au marché.** *There were a lot of people at the market.*
- Because it is used for descriptions, the imperfect tense is used to convey physical states such as weather, or emotional states such as feelings: **Il faisait beau lorsque nous étions en vacances.** *It was sunny when we were on holidays.*
- It is formed by taking the first-person plural (**nous**) form of the present tense and replacing the **-ons** ending with the following endings: **-ais, -ais, -ait, -ions, -iez, -aient**.
- The same rule applies whether a verb is regular or irregular.
- The endings for the imperfect tense are the same for all verb groups.

	Present	Imperfect
je	finis	finissais
tu	finis	finissais
il/elle	finit	finissait
nous	finissons	finissions
vous	finissez	finissiez
ils/elles	finissent	finissaient

	Present	Imperfect
je	fais	faisais
tu	fais	faisais
il/elle	fait	faisait
nous	faisons	faisions
vous	faites	faisiez
ils/elles	font	faisaient

1 Give these verbs in the first-person plural present (*nous*) and the imperfect form indicated.

E.g. venir = nous venons → vous veniez

a. partir = nous .... → je ....

b. aimer = nous .... → ils ....

c. croire = nous .... → tu ....

d. prendre = nous .... → vous ....

e. faire = nous .... → elle ....

2 **Complete each sentence with the appropriate verb in the imperfect tense. Beware, there is one too many!**

a. Il .... nuit lorsque l'avion a atterri.

b. Nous .... à la plage tous les matins ! Quelles vacances !

c. ....-vous nous voir avant de partir ?

d. Je .... très fatigué.

e. Vous .... tous ensemble ? Vous .... être à l'étroit !

me sentais — habitiez — allions — deviez — vouliez — cuisinait — faisait

3 **Conjugate these verbs in the imperfect tense.**

a. Je .... (savoir) que vous .... (être) en France !

b. Il .... (penser) que tu .... (avoir) deux chats !

c. Nous .... (avoir) les cheveux blonds quand nous .... (être) petits.

d. .... (manger)-tu des pâtes à 3 heures ce matin ?

e. Avant, Caroline .... (appeler) sa sœur tous les soirs.

Perfect or imperfect?

- The present perfect (**avoir** or **être** + past participle) is used for a one-off completed action or event in the past.
- The imperfect tense is used for actions or events that happened either on a regular basis or continuously in the past or for describing something about the past.
  J'ai vu ce film l'année dernière. (perfect)
  Lorsque j'étais jeune, j'allais au cinéma tous les samedis ! (imperfect)
- These two tenses are often used together in a sentence. The imperfect describes an ongoing action and the perfect a one-off action:
  Je dormais (imperfect) **quand tu as téléphoné** (perfect).

4 Are these sentences in the perfect or imperfect tense?

	Passé composé	Imparfait
a. *Je suis allée au théâtre.*	☐	☐
b. *Il préparait un gâteau au chocolat.*	☐	☐
c. *Nous mangions au restaurant.*	☐	☐
d. *Stéphane a vu un renard dans le pré.*	☐	☐
e. *Marie-Luce dormait à poings fermés.*	☐	☐
f. *Gwendolyne s'est promenée au parc.*	☐	☐
g. *Vous avez regardé le film hier soir ?*	☐	☐
h. *Je lisais mon livre tranquillement.*	☐	☐

5 Conjugate the verbs using either the perfect or imperfect as required.

a. Je .... **(faire)** la sieste lorsque la voisine .... **(sonner)** à la porte.

b. Lorsqu'il .... **(rentrer)**, Audrey .... **(regarder)** la télévision.

c. Il .... **(se rendre)** à la banque quand il l'a .... **(rencontrer)**.

d. Elles .... **(être)** en vacances et elles .... **(acheter)** de très jolis vêtements.

e. Le chat .... **(s'apprêter)** à bondir lorsque l'oiseau .... **(s'envoler)**.

6 Connect the two parts of the sentences that go together.

1. Je visitais l'Italie •	• **a.** quand il est tombé.
2. Je garais la voiture •	• **b.** lorsque tu t'es évanouie ?
3. Elle plantait de la menthe •	• **c.** quand la Peugeot m'est rentrée dedans !
4. Passais-tu ton examen •	• **d.** lorsque vous vous êtes rencontrés ?
5. Il redescendait la montagne •	• **e.** lorsque j'ai rencontré Lorenzo.
6. Vous faisiez du ski •	• **f.** quand elle s'est fait piquer par une araignée.

Conditional sentences

- The conditional is a verb form that is used to express what would happen if a certain condition is met. It can also be used to soften a preference or a wish or to make a polite request. In a conditional sentence, in the clause stating the condition using **si** *if*, the verb is in the imperfect tense, and the clause stating the conditional outcome is in the conditional (see tables below).

Conditional (*le conditionnel présent*)
In English, the conditional is formed using *would* + verb, but in French the verb conjugates by adding the following endings to the infinitive (for **-re** verbs, the final **-e** is dropped first). (In fact, the endings are the same as the imperfect tense: simple!)

je	regarderais
tu	regarderais
il/elle	regarderait
nous	regarderions
vous	regarderiez
ils/elles	regarderaient

je	choisirais
tu	choisirais
il/elle	choisirait
nous	choisirions
vous	choisiriez
ils/elles	choisiraient

je	vendrais
tu	vendrais
il/elle	vendrait
nous	vendrions
vous	vendriez
ils/elles	vendraient

7 **Put the verbs in these sentences in the conditional.**

a. Je .... **(partir)** en vacances demain si je le pouvais !

b. Julian .... **(finir)** sa toile s'il avait le temps !

c. Avec des « si », on .... **(mettre)** Paris en bouteille !

d. Martine .... **(préférer)** prendre le train.

e. Hélène et Simon .... **(vendre)** leur maison très vite s'ils le voulaient !

8 **Conjugate the verbs in the conditional or imperfect to form conditional sentences.**

E.g. Si je gagnais (imperfect) **au loto, j'achèterais** (conditional) **une nouvelle voiture.**

a. Si tu .... **(parler)** moins, tu .... **(finir)** plus vite !

b. Vous .... **(s'amuser)** vraiment si vous .... **(venir)** en vacances avec nous !

c. Si Luc le lui .... **(demander)**, Aline .... **(aimer)** beaucoup l'épouser !

d. Nathan .... **(être)** heureux si Julie lui ....**(écrire)** une lettre !

Irregular verbs in the conditional

The verbs **être** and **avoir** are irregular in the conditional:

être	
je	**serais**
tu	**serais**
il/elle	**serait**
nous	**serions**
vous	**seriez**
ils/elles	**seraient**

avoir	
j'	**aurais**
tu	**aurais**
il/elle	**aurait**
nous	**aurions**
vous	**auriez**
ils/elles	**auraient**

Other irregular verbs

The stem is the same as that used for the future tense to which is added the conditional endings:

aller → j'irais
devoir → je devrais
faire → je ferais
pouvoir → je pourrais
savoir → je saurais
venir → je viendrais
voir → je verrais
vouloir → je voudrais

9 Use the correct conditional verb in each of the sentences.

a. Je .... mieux si tu allumais la lumière !

b. Lucas .... arrêter de courir : il semble essoufflé.

c. Il .... un miracle pour que Béatrice fasse ses devoirs !

d. Il .... la course s'il avait plus confiance en lui.

e. Il fait si chaud, Louise .... tout ce qu'elle a pour une glace !

f. Nous .... déjà arrivés s'il n'y avait pas tant de circulation.

faudrait
gagnerait
verrais
serions
devrait
donnerait

10 Conjugate these verbs in the imperfect, perfect or conditional depending on the context.

a. Je .... (préparer) le dîner lorsque Samuel .... (arriver).

b. Si tu .... (faire) un effort, tu y .... (arriver) !

c. Vous .... (voir) la chenille si vous .... (regarder) de plus près.

d. Nous ne .... (pouvoir) pas comprendre, même si nous .... (essayer).

e. J' .... (écouter) la radio lorsque la nouvelle.................. (tomber).

Génial ! You've completed Lesson 12! It's time to count up the icons for the exercises and record your result here and in the table on page 128.

13
Prepositions

What is a preposition?

- A preposition gives spatial or temporal details about something (usually a noun, noun phrase or pronoun). It shows the relationship of its object to the rest of the sentence: **Il se cache <u>derrière</u> l'arbre.**
- They can be single words (**à, dans, sur**) or phrases (**à côté de, en dessous de**).
- Some prepositions can be used as adverbs: **Il l'a rangé <u>dessous</u>**.

1 Underline the prepositions in the following sentences.

a. Anne et Marie se sont cachées sous la table !

b. Vas-tu chez tes parents à Pâques ?

c. Edwige part à Tours avec ses enfants cet après-midi.

d. Guy est allé dans la forêt cueillir des champignons.

e. Elles sont parties pendant une heure.

Prepositions with geographical terms (cities, countries, continents)

To say *to* or *in* + geographical term, you need to know the gender of the location. Most geographical terms ending in **-e** are feminine, although there are a few exceptions. The table below shows which preposition or preposition/article contraction to use.

No article (e.g. for cities)	**à**	**Paris** **Barcelone** **Londres**
Masculine and starts with a consonant	**au**	**Japon** **Portugal**
Masculine and starts with a vowel Feminine	**en**	**Europe** **Asie** **Suède** **Afrique**
Plural	**aux**	**États-Unis**

2 Complete the sentences using *à*, *au*, *en* or *aux*.

a. Nous allons .... Brésil le mois prochain !

b. Julien voudrait se rendre .... Inde pour les vacances.

c. Nadia vit .... Émirats Arabes Unis.

d. Pablo est-il né .... Espagne ou .... Portugal ?

e. J'adorerais passer Noël .... îles Fidji !

f. Kate retourne bientôt .... Angleterre.

g. Tu vas .... Lille après-demain ?

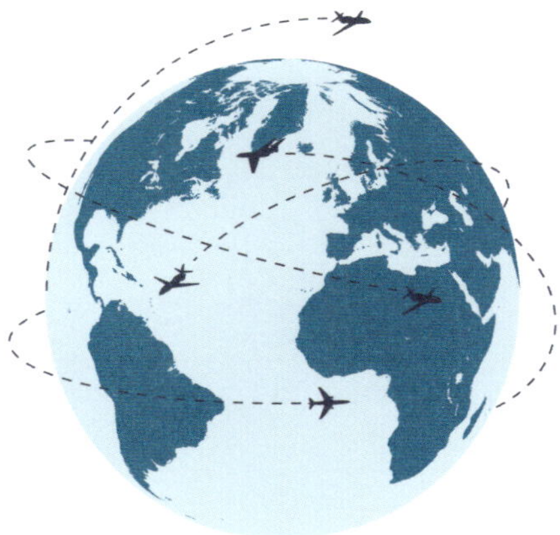

3 Use the terms to construct sentences as in the example.

E.g. Emilia / Varsovie / Pologne : Emilia vit à Varsovie, en Pologne.

a. Aden / Marrakech / Maroc ....

b. Acha / Yaoundé / Cameroun ....

c. Éléanore / Besançon / France ....

d. Aiko / Tokyo / Japon ....

e. Eeva / Helsinki / Finlande ....

Prepositions and adverbs of place (*Les prépositions et adverbes de lieu*)

- Prepositions of place are used to give information about where something is.
- Adverbs of place tell where something happened (i.e. the location of the action of the verb). They are usually placed after the verb: **Qu'est-ce que tu fais en haut ?**

PREPOSITIONS	ADVERBS	English
dans, en	**dedans**	*in, within, into, inside*
sur, au-dessus de	**dessus, au-dessus**	*on, on top (of), over, above*
sous, en dessous de	**dessous, en dessous**	*under, below*
à côté de	**à côté**	*next to, beside*
devant	**devant**	*in front of*
derrière	**derrière, à l'arrière**	*behind, in back of*
entre	-	*between*
parmi	-	*among*
contre	**contre**	*against*
près de	**(tout) près**	*near*
loin de	**loin**	*far, a long way from*
en face de	**en face**	*opposite, across*
au milieu de	**au milieu**	*in the middle (of)*
à droite de	**à droite**	*to the right (of)*
à gauche de	**à gauche**	*to the left (of)*
en bas de	**en bas**	*down from, at the bottom*
en haut de	**en haut**	*up from, at the top*
vers	-	*towards, in the direction of*

4 **Underline the most appropriate preposition in each sentence according to the context.**

a. La balle est tombée **en bas des / au milieu des / en haut des** escaliers.

b. Le poulet est **sous / dans / sur** le frigo.

c. Oh non ! Le chat de la voisine est coincé **en bas de / au milieu de / en haut de** l'arbre ! Il ne pourra jamais redescendre tout seul !

d. Ton cochon d'Inde se cache encore **sous / sur / à côté du** le canapé : il va être difficile de l'attraper !

e. Pourquoi as-tu garé la voiture **devant / dessus / dessous** le garage et non pas dedans ?

5 Use the table on the left to complete each sentence with the most appropriate preposition.

a. Le restaurant est-il .... la maison ? Je n'ai pas envie de marcher trop longtemps !

b. La boulangerie se trouve .... la boucherie et le café.

c. Les toilettes sont tout de suite .... escaliers ; vous montez et c'est à votre droite.

d. Je crois que le gâteau est .... la table de la cuisine.

e. Ne te retourne pas ! Il y a une énorme araignée .... toi !

6 Preposition or adverb of place? Underline the correct choice.

a. As-tu mis ma chemise **dans / dedans** le sac de voyage ?
– Oui, elle est **dans / dedans** !

b. Regarde ! Hélène est assise **à côté de / à côté** Sébastien !

c. Où est garée la moto ?
– Elle est garée là, **à gauche de / à gauche**.

d. Les clés sont **en dessous de / en dessous** la valise.

e. Oh non ! La maison est encore **loin de / loin** !

Is it *à* or *chez*?

The preposition **à** *to, at, in* can be used with any location. In contrast, **chez** always refers to a place related to a person, e.g. at someone's house, office, etc.

à + place	**à l'école** **à la piscine** **au restaurant**
chez + person	**chez Christophe** **chez mes parents** **chez le dentiste**

7 Complete the sentences with *à / l' / à la / au / aux / chez.*

a. Je suis arrivé en retard .... école ce matin.

b. Vas-tu .... fête du village samedi prochain ?

c. Ils sont allés .... Caroline hier soir.

d. Stéphanie a rendez-vous .... le médecin vendredi matin à 9h30.

e. Elles sont arrivées .... urgences vers minuit.

f. Il vient d'arriver .... bureau.

à and de

- **à** is used to indicate that you are going somewhere: **Je vais à la gare.** *I am going to the station.*
- **de** is used to indicate that you are coming from somewhere: **Je viens de la pharmacie.** *I am coming from the pharmacy.*

8 Connect each phrase to the correct verb.

à l'école.

de la boîte de nuit !

aux vendanges !

1. Je vais

2. Je sors

du cours de guitare.

du cinéma.

à la pêche avec mon frère !

de l'opéra.

au mariage de Maé et Joris.

Temporal prepositions (*Les prépositions de temps*)

• **dans / en**

In reference to time, both prepositions mean *in*, but are used differently: **dans** indicates the amount of time before something will occur in the future, whereas **en** indicates how long an action takes: **Noah arrive dans 10 minutes.** *Noah will arrive in ten minutes.* (He will be here ten minutes from now.) **Noah a lu le journal en dix minutes.** *Noah read the newspaper in ten minutes.* (It took him 10 minutes to read it.) Also, **en** introduces the date or time of an event: **Tom part en vacances en août.** *Tom is going on holiday in August.*

• **depuis**

This preposition can mean *since* or *for*. It indicates the duration of time of something still taking place: **Il court depuis 20 minutes.** *He has been running for 20 minutes.* **Je chante depuis 2015.** *I've been singing since 2015.*

• **pendant / durant**

This also refers to duration (*during, for, while*) but in the past or future: **Il a couru pendant 20 minutes.** *He ran for 20 minutes.* **Il se reposera pendant l'été.** *He will rest during the summer.*

9 **Complete the sentences with the correct preposition: *pendant, depuis, dans* or *en*.**

a. Nous allons aller à la plage .... les vacances ! Youpi !

b. Dépêche-toi ! Le train arrive .... une heure !

c. Il habite à Paris .... 2002.

d. La famille Charlet déménage .... septembre.

e. Ils parlent .... des heures quand Jonathan téléphone !

f. Il fait beau .... le début de l'été.

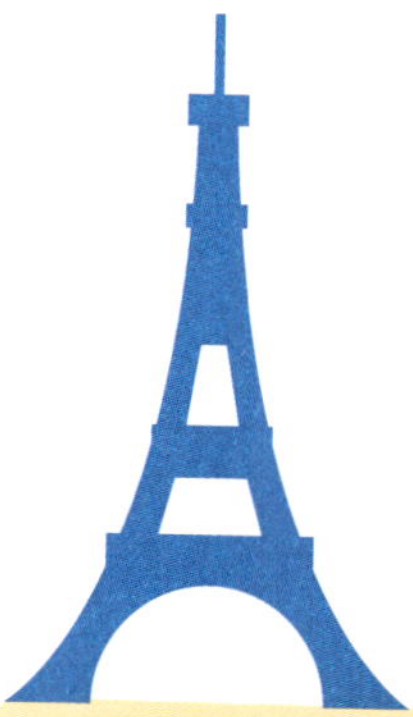

Other temporal prepositions

à partir de, dès *from, starting from*
après *after*
avant *before*
de … à … *from … to …*
entre *between*
il y a *ago*
il y a … que … *for*
jusqu'à *until*
pour *for*
vers *around, at about*

10 Fill in the crossword with the French temporal prepositions according to the English clues.

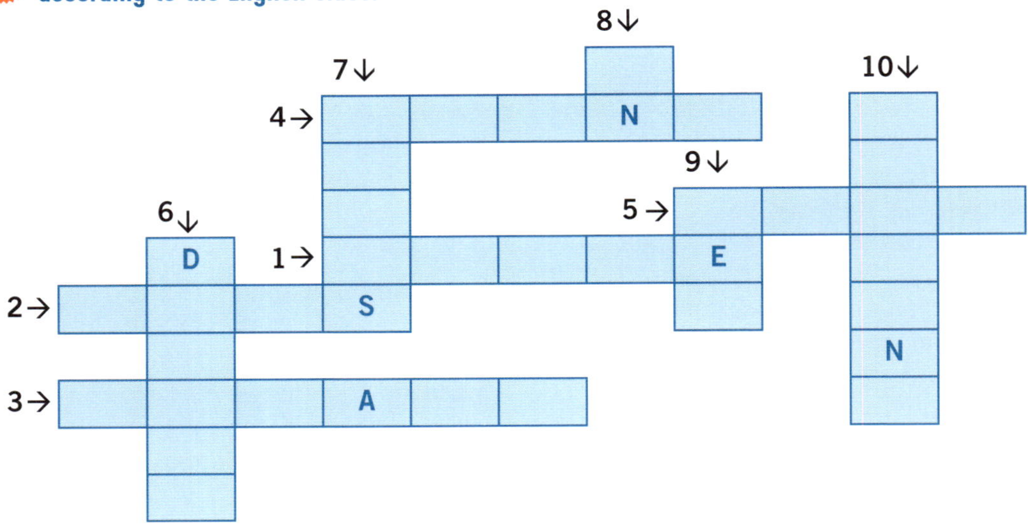

Across
1. between
2. towards
3. during
4. before
5. in

Down
6. since
7. after
8. in
9. as soon as
10. during, while

11 Match each French preposition with its English equivalent.

1. au sujet de, à propos de •	• a. *in spite of*
2. avec •	• b. *as for*
3. contre •	• c. *against*
4. malgré •	• d. *with*
5. par •	• e. *except*
6. quant à •	• f. *about*
7. sans •	• g. *according to*
8. sauf •	• h. *by*
9. selon •	• i. *without*

Verbs + prepositions

Certain verbs are always followed by a specific preposition, most frequently **de** or **à**. It is wise to memorize the preposition with the verb when you learn it. Here are a few common examples:

- verb + **à** + noun/pronoun

assister à *to attend or be present (e.g. at an event)*
demander à *to ask (someone)*
faire attention à *to pay attention to*
s'intéresser à *to be interested in*
jouer à *to play (a sport)*
participer à *to participate (in something)*
penser à *to think of/about*
téléphoner à *to phone (someone)*

- verb + **à** + infinitive

aider à *to help to*
apprendre à *to learn to*
arriver à *to manage to*
commencer à *to begin to*
demander à *to ask to*
hésiter à *to hesitate to*
réussir à *to succeed in*

- verb + **de** + noun/pronoun

changer de *to change*
jouer de *to play an instrument*
partir de *to leave from*
s'approcher de *to approach*
se moquer de *to make fun of*
s'occuper de *to be busy with*
se rendre compte de *to realize*
se souvenir de *to remember*

- verb + **de** + infinitive

avoir peur de *to be afraid to*
cesser de *to stop (doing something)*
décider de *to decide to*
essayer de *to try to*
finir de *to finish*
oublier de *to forget to*
permettre de *to allow to*

12 Complete the sentences with the correct preposition: *à / au / à l' / aux* or *de / du / de la / des.*

a. Fais attention .... trous ! Ne tombe pas !

b. Julian joue .... la guitare.

c. Ah enfin ! Tu commences .... comprendre cet exercice !

d. Fais demi-tour ! J'ai oublié .... fermer la porte d'entrée !

e. Je me souviens .... jour où la foudre est tombée sur ta maison ! Quelle frayeur !

Formidable ! You've completed Lesson 13! It's time to count up the icons for the exercises and record your results here and in the table on page 128.

14

Adverbs

Forming adverbs

- An adverb is a word or a phrase that modifies the meaning of an adjective, verb or other adverb. They can express manner, place, time or degree: **Elle court vite.** *She runs fast.*
- Some adverbs (especially of manner) can be formed by adding the suffix **-ment** to an adjective. The suffix is added to the masculine form of an adjective ending in a vowel (**rapide → rapidement)** or to the feminine form of an adjective ending in a consonant **(lent → lente → lentement)**. There are some exceptions to this rule: **bref → brièvement, gentil → gentiment**.
- Adjectives ending in **-ant / -ent** change to **-amment / -emment**: **courant → couramment**, **patient → patiemment**.
- A few other adverbs end in **-ément** such as **précisément** or **énormément**.

1 Turn these adjectives into adverbs.

a. prudent = ...

b. joli = ...

c. malheureux = ...

d. constant = ...

e. gentil = ...

f. joyeux = ...

g. profond = ...

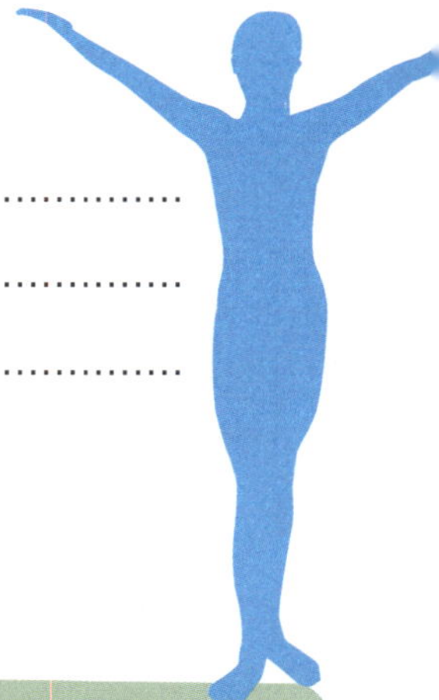

Word order

- In French, an adverb usually comes after the verb it modifies. Long adverbs usually come after the past participle in a perfect tense: **Julie est rentrée rapidement.** *Julie came home quickly.* But, **certainement, complètement, probablement** are exceptions and come before the past participle: **Tu as probablement mangé.**
- Shorter adverbs, such as **bien, souvent, mal, beaucoup**, also come before the past participle: **J'ai bien mangé !**
- An adverb modifying the meaning of an adjective or another adverb is placed before it: **Elle est vraiment jolie.**
- With a negative verb, adverbs are placed after **pas**: **Elle dort bien. > Elle ne dort pas bien.**

2 Put the words in order to make sentences.

a. Tellement / Luc / est / fatigué = ...

b. pas / souvent / vais / ne / théâtre / Je / au = ...

c. beaucoup / a / cette / grandi / année / Il = ...

d. Vous / gentils / très / êtes = ...

e. Il / maison / entré / silencieusement / la / dans / est = ...

Adverbs of manner

- French adverbs of manner mostly end in **-ment** (e.g. **rapidement, sérieuse-ment, lentement, gentiment**).
- There are a few very frequently used adverbs of manner that do not follow this pattern:

Adjective	Adverb
bon → *good*	**bien** → *well*
mauvais → *bad*	**mal** → *badly*
meilleur → *better*	**mieux** → *better*

3 Underline the correct word in each context.

a. C'est le **mieux / meilleur** film de l'année !

b. Louis m'a posé la question **gentil / gentiment**.

c. Est-ce un **bon / bien** dessert ?

d. Vous allez **bon / bien** ?

e. Karine va beaucoup **mieux / meilleur** aujourd'hui.

Adverbs of frequency (*Les adverbes de fréquence*)

These are usually placed after the verb.

- -	**jamais**	*never*
-	**rarement**	*rarely*
+	**quelquefois** **parfois** **de temps en temps**	*sometimes* *occasionally* *at times*
+ +	**souvent** **généralement**	*often* *generally*
+ + +	**toujours** **tout le temps**	*always* *all the time*

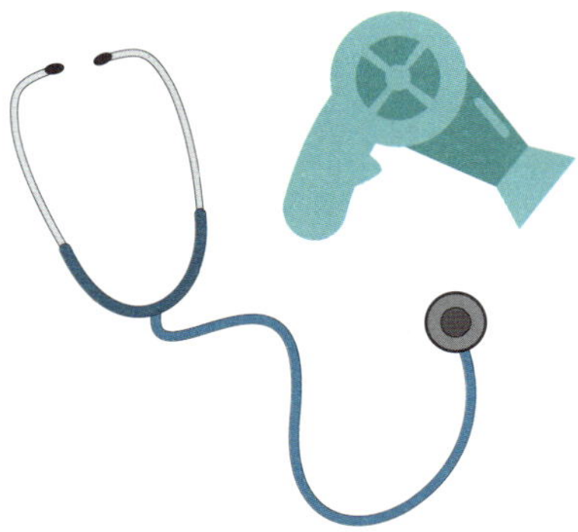

4 Underline the appropriate adverb of frequency according to the context.

a. **Homme d'affaires** : Je pars **parfois / souvent** en voyage.

b. **Professeur des écoles** : Je travaille **quelquefois / toujours** avec des enfants.

c. **Fermier** : Je travaille **parfois / toujours** avec un ordinateur.

d. **Médecin généraliste** : Je rencontre **parfois / souvent** des gens.

e. **Coiffeur :** Je bavarde **rarement / généralement** avec mes clients.

5 Choose the appropriate adverb to complete each sentence according to the context.

a. Le cinéma ? Il déteste ça. Il n'y va ....

b. L'opéra ? C'est tellement cher ! Elle n'y va que très ....

c. La télévision ? Nous adorons ! Nous regardons .... les programmes du soir ensemble !

d. Le théâtre ? Oui, cela lui arrive d'y aller. Pas très .... mais .... il y a un spectacle intéressant.

e. À quelle heure sort-elle du bureau ? Elle en sort .... à 16h30.

rarement
généralement
jamais
quelquefois
toujours
souvent

Adverbs of time / Temporal adverbs (*Les adverbes de temps*)

Adverbs of time that answer the question **Quand ?** *When?* can be placed at the beginning or the end of a sentence: **Aujourd'hui, je pars en vacances. / Je pars en vacances aujourd'hui.**

actuellement *currently*
après *after*
après-demain *the day after tomorrow*
aujourd'hui *today*
auparavant *previously*
autrefois *in the past*
avant *before*
avant-hier *the day before yesterday*
bientôt *soon*
déjà *already*
demain *tomorrow*
depuis *since*
enfin *finally*
ensuite *next*
hier *yesterday*
il y a *ago*
jamais *never*
longtemps *a long time*
maintenant *now*
parfois *sometimes*
puis *then*
rarement *rarely*
souvent *often*
tard *late*
tôt *early*
toujours *always, still*
tout de suite *immediately*

6 **Complete the sentences with the appropriate adverbs of time from the list above.**

a. Mets ton réveil à 5 heures du matin : nous devons nous lever ....

b. Des nuages sont apparus, ... le vent s'est levé.

c. Rex ! Viens ici .... ! Quelle bêtise as-tu encore faite ?

d. Ne pleure pas Edwige, ta maman va rentrer .... Plus que cinq minutes et elle sera là.

e. J'ai rencontré Carla .... cinq ans et nous ne nous sommes pas quittés depuis !

f. J'adore ce parc ; je viens .... ici.

g. Joshua n'aime pas les carottes. J'en cuisine ....

Adverbs of place

Adverbs of place usually come after the direct object. They answer the question **Où ?** *Where?*

à droite *to the right*
à gauche *to the left*
à l'intérieur de *inside*
autour *around*
dedans *inside*
dehors *outside*
derrière *behind*
devant *in front*
en bas *downstairs, at the bottom*
en haut *upstairs, at the top*
ici *here*
là *there*
là-bas *over there*
loin *far*
nulle part *nowhere*
partout *everywhere*
près *near*
quelque part *somewhere*

7 Complete the sentences using the appropriate adverb of place shown at the right.

a. As-tu vu Domino ? – Non, je l'ai cherché .... mais je ne l'ai trouvé ....

b. Je dois passer l'aspirateur. Allez donc jouer .... avec le ballon !

c. Finalement, j'ai cherché Domino dehors et il était .... !

d. Ton revers est incroyable ! Mais où est la balle ?
– Je la vois ! Elle est ...., à côté des arbres !
– Elle est vraiment .... !

e. Victor ? Où es-tu ? Je suis à l'étage et je ne te trouve pas !
– Mais, je ne suis pas à l'étage, je suis .... !

Adverbs of quantity

Adverbs of quantity explain how much of something there is:

beaucoup (de) *a lot (of)*
assez (de) *enough*
peu (de) *little, few*
trop (de) *too much, too many*
plus (de) *more*
un peu (de) *a little*

- These are often followed by **de** + noun (without an article).

8 Complete the sentences with the appropriate adverb of quantity shown to the left.

a. Beurk, mon café est dégoûtant ! Il y a .... sucre.

b. Arrêtez ! Merci, ça suffira. Il y a .... lait dans mon café.

c. Le café était calme. Il y avait très .... gens présents.

d. Désirez-vous autre chose, Madame ? – Oui, j'aimerais .... sucre dans mon café, s'il vous plaît.

e. Je ne sais que choisir ! Il y a .... gâteaux et ils sont tous appétissants !

Interrogative adverbs

Interrogative adverbs are used to ask questions:

Combien (de) ? *How much? / How many?*
Comment ? *How?*
Où ? *Where?*
Pourquoi ? *Why?*
Quand ? *When?*
Quel ? *Which?*
Qui ? *Who?*

9 Use the appropriate interrogative adverb for each of these questions.

a. .... est Thomas ? – Il est dans sa chambre.

b. .... es-tu allé à Dijon ? – J'y suis allé en train.

c. .... est avec Florence ? – C'est Laurent, son cousin.

d. .... venez-vous nous voir ? – Nous venons le mois prochain, c'est promis !

e. .... es-tu en colère ? – Oh, cet imbécile m'a pris ma place de parking !

10 Complete each sentence with the appropriate adverb of time, manner, place or quantity.

a. On ne risque pas d'avoir un accident : ma grand-mère conduit si .... !

b. Il va .... au travail en vélo. Il adore le grand air !

c. Je pense que cette réponse est correcte : tu as .... raison.

d. Je déteste le poisson ! Je n'en mange ....

e. .... , Jennifer et Océane ne pourront pas venir à ton anniversaire.

f. Julien est .... très généreux.

g. Vous n'avez pas besoin de répéter ; j'ai .... compris.

Oui ! You have completed Lesson 14. It's time to count up the icons for the exercises and record your results here and in the table on page 128.

15
More on verbs

Modal verbs

A modal verb is used to express likelihood, ability, permission or obligation (e.g. *can, should, must*, etc.). The construction is: conjugated modal verb + infinitive.

- **devoir** expresses obligation: *to have to (should, ought to, must).*

je	dois
tu	dois
il/elle	doit
nous	devons
vous	devez
ils/elles	doivent

- **pouvoir** expresses ability, possibility and permission: *to be able to (can).*

je	peux
tu	peux
il/elle	peut
nous	pouvons
vous	pouvez
ils/elles	peuvent

- Note: when inverted in a question, **je peux** becomes **puis-je**: **Puis-je me laver les mains ?**

- **vouloir** expresses desire: *to want to* (it also exists as an independent verb).

je	veux
tu	veux
il/elle	veut
nous	voulons
vous	voulez
ils/elles	veulent

1 Complete the sentences with the correct modal verb.

a. ....-vous aller à l'école demain ?

b. Nous ne .... pas manger ou boire ici.

c. ....-je utiliser les toilettes, s'il vous plaît ?

d. Elles .... rentrer à 10 heures.

e. Tu .... venir avec nous au cinéma ?

f. Il .... visiter l'Écosse.

veux
pouvons
doivent
veut
puis
devez

2 Conjugate these modal verbs in the present tense.

a. Maman, Camille .... **(pouvoir)** venir à la maison cet après-midi ?

b. Vous .... **(devoir)** ôter vos chaussures avant d'entrer.

c. Je .... **(devoir)** étudier pour cet examen !

d. Nous .... **(devoir)** faire les courses pour le week-end.

e. Chut ! Elles .... **(pouvoir)** nous entendre !

Impersonal verbs

These are verbs in which the subject is not directly specified. This avoids naming who or what is 'responsible' for the action. The verb always conjugates in the third-person singular.

- **falloir** *to be necessary, to have to*: **Il faut partir.** *We need to go.* **Il faudrait prévoir.** *You should plan ahead.*
- **valoir (mieux)** *to be worth it, to be better to*: **Il vaut mieux utiliser la porte !** *It's better to use the door!*
- Expressions describing the weather are impersonal as they don't directly specify the subject: **Il pleut. Il fait beau.**
- **il y a** *there is/there are* is another very frequent impersonal expression: **Il y a beaucoup de monde.**
- **il paraît que** *it appears that* **/ il semble que** *it seems that* **/ on dirait que** *one might say that*: **Il semble qu'il va pleuvoir.**

3 Connect the statements that go together.

1. Sortez les skis ! •	• **a.** Il pleut !
2. Je dois trouver mon parapluie ! •	• **b.** Il fait beau !
3. Il faut mettre les manteaux ! •	• **c.** Il fait chaud !
4. Nous pouvons sortir en t-shirt ! •	• **d.** Il neige !
5. Peux-tu me donner un verre d'eau ? •	• **e.** Il fait froid !

4 Translate the following sentences into French.

a. It is necessary to go to school.

→ ....

b. The weather is beautiful today!

→ ....

c. It's summer! It's very hot.

→ ....

d. It's worthwile having a mobile phone.

→ ....

e. There are not many people here.

→ ....

When 'to be' is not *être*

Some phrases expressed with 'to be' in English use **avoir** in French:

to be hungry **avoir faim**
to be thirsty **avoir soif**
to be hot **avoir chaud**
to be cold **avoir froid**
to be right **avoir raison**
to be wrong **avoir tort**
to be lucky **avoir de la chance**
to be … years old **avoir … ans**

5 Translate the following sentences into English.

a. As-tu froid ? ➜ ……………………………………………………………

b. J'ai très faim. ➜ ……………………………………………………………

c. Nous avons tort. ➜ ……………………………………………………………

d. J'ai 41 ans. ➜ ……………………………………………………………

e. Vous avez de la chance. ➜ ……………………………………………………………

6 Translate the following sentences into French.

a. You are right! It is raining!

➜ ……………………………………………………………

b. I am really cold! Close the window!

➜ ……………………………………………………………

c. We are lucky! We won!

➜ ……………………………………………………………

d. How old is she? – She is 26.

➜ ……………………………………………………………

e. Are you hungry?

➜ ……………………………………………………………

Transitive and intransitive verbs

• A **transitive verb** is a verb that can take a direct object (i.e. someone or something directly receives the action of the verb).

Subject	Transitive verb	Direct object
J'ai	mangé	un croissant.

• Note: when the direct object is a pronoun, it is usually placed in front of the verb.

Subject	Direct object	Transitive verb
Je	la	vois.

• An **intransitive verb** does not take a direct object. It can, however, take an indirect object (someone or something that indirectly receives the action of the verb). It is often followed by a preposition (e.g. **à**). Some verbs are intransitive by nature (**pleurer, nager, voyager,** etc.).

Subject	Intransitive verb	Indirect object
Nous	parlons	aux voisins.

7 Underline the verbs in these sentences and tick whether they are transitive (T) or intransitive (I).

	T	I
a. Nous mangeons une pizza tous les vendredis.	☐	☐
b. Sabine écoute une chanson.	☐	☐
c. Corinne parle à ses amis.	☐	☐
d. Tu réponds à tante Colette ?	☐	☐
e. Je bois du café tous les matins.	☐	☐

8 Underline the objects in these sentences and tick whether they are direct (D) or indirect (I).

	D	I
a. J'ai donné mon livre.	☐	☐
b. Elle téléphone à Alice.	☐	☐
c. Nous écrivons à nos parents.	☐	☐
d. Tu chantes cette chanson.	☐	☐
e. Nous pensons à nos vacances.	☐	☐

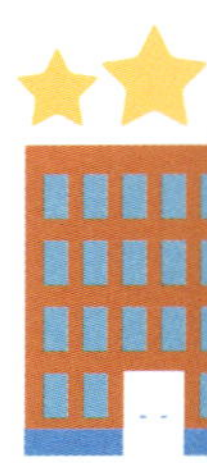

Present participles

- This verb form conveys a continuous action: in English it ends in *-ing*. To form the present participle, use the first-person plural (**nous**) form of the present tense and replace **-ons** with the ending **-ant**: **nous regardons** *we look* → **regardant** *looking*.

parler → **nous parlons** → drop **-ons**, add **-ant** → **parlant**

vendre → **nous vendons** → drop **-ons**, add **-ant** → **vendant**

prendre → **nous prenons** → drop **-ons**, add **-ant** → **prenant**

finir → **nous finissons** → drop **-ons**, add **-ant** → **finissant**

ranger → **nous rangeons** → drop **-ons**, add **-ant** → **rangeant**

faire → **nous faisons** → drop **-ons**, add **-ant** → **faisant**

- Here are two important irregular forms:

avoir → **ayant**

être → **étant**

- The present participle is used essentially in French with the preposition **en** meaning *on*, *upon*, *while*, *by*: **en regardant la télé** *while watching TV*, **en faisant ce travail** *by doing this work*. It is also sometimes used as an adjective.

9 Give the present participle of these verbs.

a. lancer → ....

b. aimer → ....

c. acheter → ....

d. voir → ....

e. maigrir → ....

f. venir → ....

g. s'habiller → ....

Bravo ! You've completed Lesson 15. It's time to count up the icons for the exercises and record your results here and in the table on page 128.

16 Linking words

Linking words

- These are transition words used to connect words or clauses, showing the relationship between them. They are called **conjunctions *(les conjonctions)*** and include words such as *and, but, or, however, because*, etc. There are two types: coordinating and subordinating conjunctions.
- **Coordinating conjunctions *(Les conjonctions de coordination)***
  Coordinating conjunctions connect words, clauses or sentences that are independent and grammatically equal.
- Some of the most common coordinating conjunctions are:

d'ailleurs *besides*
ainsi *thus*
à savoir *that is to say*
au contraire *on the contrary*
aussi *also*
car *because*
c'est-à-dire *that is to say*
c'est pourquoi *that's why*
cependant *nonetheless*
donc *therefore, consequently*
en effet *indeed*
et *and*
mais *but*
néanmoins *nevertheless*
ni … ni… *neither… nor*
or *however*
ou *or*
pourtant *yet*
soit … soit … *either … or…*
toutefois *nevertheless*

1 Underline the coordinating conjunctions in these sentences.

a. Je suis passé chez toi, mais tu n'étais pas là.
b. Soit tu viens avec nous, soit tu ne viens pas ; mais, s'il te plaît, décide-toi !
c. Marion pense cuisiner un bœuf bourguignon ou un navarin.
d. La voiture est au garage donc je ne pourrai pas venir te voir ce matin. Désolé !
e. Je ne me sens pas très bien, cependant j'essaierai d'aller en cours.

2 Complete the sentences with the appropriate coordinating conjunction.

car – c'est pourquoi – au contraire – pourtant – donc – cependant

a. Julien pose des questions …………… il va falloir répondre.
b. Laetitia n'aime pas skier, ……………. elle reste au chalet.
c. Florian ne s'énerve jamais, …………. il reste toujours serein.
d. Marine n'aime pas le chocolat, …….. elle a fait un effort et a goûté ton gâteau.
e. Maxime lui fait confiance, ………….. il a un doute.
f. Je suis au lit ……………………………. je suis malade.

Subordinating conjunctions (*Les conjonctions de subordination*)

- These are conjunctions that connect a subordinate clause to a main clause.
- A subordinate clause is a phrase that is dependent on a main clause. It doesn't make sense on its own, but gives more information about the main clause. Typically, a subordinate clause is introduced by a subordinating conjunction that links it to the main clause.

Je l'aime bien	**parce qu'elle m'a aidé.**
I like her	*because she helped me.*
Main clause	Subordinate clause

- Some of the most common subordinating conjunctions are:

alors que *while*
à moins que *unless*
afin que *in order that, so that*
après que *after*
au cas où *in case*
aussitôt que *as soon as*
avant que *before*
bien que *although*
comme *as, since*
de peur que *for fear that*
depuis que *since*
dès que *as soon as*
jusqu'à ce que *until*
lorsque *when, at the time when*
maintenant que *now that*
parce que *because*
pendant que *while*
pour que *in order that*
pourvu que *provided that*
puisque *since*
quand *when*
que *that*
quoi que *whatever, no matter what*
quoique *although*
sans que *unless*
si *if*
tandis que *while, whereas*

3 Underline the subordinating conjunctions in these sentences.

a. Claudette a pris un parapluie au cas où il pleuve.

b. Bien que Pierre ait peur de l'eau, ils sont allés en vacances au bord de la mer.

c. Comme les enfants n'aiment pas la télévision, j'ai apporté des jeux de société.

d. Je partirai lorsque le film sera fini.

e. Depuis que j'ai 18 ans, je me sens beaucoup plus libre !

4 **Use the list on the previous page to find the synonym of each subordinating conjunction.**

a. aussitôt que ....

b. comme ....

c. lorsque ....

d. bien que ....

The subjunctive after conjunctions

See Lesson 18 on **The present subjunctive**

5 **Conjugate these verbs in the indicative or subjunctive based on what the conjunction requires.**

a. Depuis que je .... **(être)** à la retraite, la vie est belle !

b. Si tu .... **(aller)** en ville demain, préviens-moi ! J'irai avec toi.

c. Bien que les chiens me .... **(faire)** peur, je trouve celui-ci très mignon !

d. Quand tu .... **(arriver)**, nous irons voir grand-mère.

e. Quoi que nous .... **(dire)**, ils n'en feront qu'à leur tête.

6 **Match these French linking words with their English counterparts.**

GIVING THE SEQUENCE OF EVENTS

premièrement / d'abord / tout d'abord	•	•	*in the first place*
en premier lieu	•	•	*then*
deuxièmement	•	•	*firstly*
ensuite / puis	•	•	*secondly*

7 **Match these French linking words with their English counterparts.**

PRESENTING ALTERNATIVES

d'un côté… de l'autre	•	•	*in addition*
d'une part… d'autre part…	•	•	*moreover*
ou… ou…	•	•	*on the one hand … on the other*
par ailleurs	•	•	*on the one hand … on the other*
en outre	•	•	*either … or*

OPPOSING IDEAS

d'un autre côté •	• *on the other hand*
par contre •	• *on the other hand*
en revanche •	• *in contrast*
au contraire •	• *on the contrary*

8 **Match the French linking words with their English counterparts.**

GIVING EXAMPLES

ainsi •	• *for example*
par exemple •	• *in this way*
notamment •	• *in particular*
en particulier •	• *particularly*

9 **Match the French linking words with their English counterparts.**

CONCLUDING

finalement / enfin •	• *to conclude*
en conclusion / pour conclure •	• *in short*
en résumé •	• *lastly*
en bref •	• *finally*
pour finir •	• *to summarize / to sum up*

10 **Complete the sentences with the appropriate linking word.**

a. .... tu pourrais penser à quelques prénoms pour le bébé, mais ...., tu pourrais attendre qu'il soit né et décider à ce moment-là.

b. Je n'aime pas certains gâteaux : .... , le mille-feuille ou le tiramisu.

c. ...., j'aimerais présenter le sujet de ma dissertation.

d. D'abord on travaille ; ...., on s'amuse !

e. Elle a pris son parapluie ; elle sera .... protégée de la pluie.

Congratulations! You've reached the end of Lesson 16! It's time to count up the icons for the exercises and record your result here and in the table on page 128.

17 The passive voice

The passive

- In the active voice, the subject performs the action of the verb.
- In the passive voice, the emphasis is on the action rather than who carried it out. What is affected by the action becomes the subject, and the agent becomes the object.
- The passive voice is formed in French in the same way as in English, i.e. with **être** + past participle.
- This is sometimes followed by **par** *by* + agent of the action. Some verbs that are often used in the passive voice can be followed by **de** instead of **par** (**aimer, admirer, apprécier, adorer, détester, respecter, accompagner, fatiguer, entourer**, etc.): **Il est apprécié de ses élèves. Je suis accompagné de ma famille.**
- The past participle must agree in number and gender with the subject!

Active voice	**Zazie interprète cette chanson.**	*Zazie sings this song.*
Passive voice	**Cette chanson est interprétée par Zazie.**	*This song is sung by Zazie.*

1 Active or passive voice? Tick the correct column.

	Active	Passive
a. La vaisselle est faite par Joël.	☐	☐
b. Catherine range le garage.	☐	☐
c. Le chat est brossé par Manon.	☐	☐
d. Cette lettre est écrite par mon arrière-grand-mère !	☐	☐
e. Mon père a peint cette toile.	☐	☐

2 Conjugate *être* in the present tense in the following passive sentences.

a. Notre maison .... construite par notre oncle qui est architecte.

b. Les haricots .... plantés par Julien.

c. Nous .... accueillis très chaleureusement par nos amis.

d. Vous .... poursuivis par les petits voisins !

e. Tu .... invitée par Ella.

3 Complete these sentences with *être* conjugated in the present tense + past participle.

a. Ces tartes .... (être + préparer) par la classe 3e D.

b. L'arbre de Noël .... (être + décorer) par les enfants.

c. Le président français .... (être + accueillir) par le premier ministre anglais.

d. Les voleurs .... (être + arrêter) par la police.

e. Les commandes .... (être + prendre) par la serveuse.

4 Complete these sentences with *être* conjugated in the present perfect + past participle.

a. Cette sculpture .... (être + réaliser) par Auguste Rodin.

b. Ce livre .... (être + écrire) par Victor Hugo.

c. La voiture .... (être + vendre) par mon frère.

d. Ces crevettes .... (être + préparer) par maman.

e. Le ciel .... (être + illuminer) par la foudre.

Avoiding the passive

- The passive is used less in French than in English. It is more common to use the two following constructions.
- The subject pronoun **on**
  To avoid expressing a specific agent of the action, it is very common to use **on** *one* + the third-person singular verb in the active voice: **On m'a dit que tu venais à la fête samedi !** ('One told me that you were coming ...')
- The reflexive pronoun **se**
  When the agent of the action is not important or relevant, passive constructions using the reflexive pronoun **se** are sometimes used: **Les glaces se vendent très bien avec cette chaleur.** *Ice cream sells very well in this heat.* ('The ice-creams themselves sell very well ...')

5 **Transform the passive voice into the active voice using the personal pronoun *on*.**

E.g. Les clés ont été retrouvées. → On a retrouvé les clés.

a. Le bateau a été réparé. → .... le bateau.

b. Le numéro a été changé. → .... le numéro.

c. Le magasin a été ouvert. → .... le magasin.

d. Le vase a été cassé. → .... le vase.

e. La maison a été bâtie. → .... la maison.

6 **Conjugate these verbs with the reflexive pronoun to put these sentences in the passive voice.**

a. Comment cela .... (se dire)-il en anglais ?

b. Le vin blanc .... (se servir) très frais.

c. Cela ne .... (se faire) pas. Ce n'est pas poli.

d. Ce plat .... (se manger) chaud et accompagné de haricots blancs.

e. Les toilettes .... (se trouver) au fond du couloir.

7 **Transform the active voice into the passive voice using *être* in the perfect tense + past participle.**

a. Caroline a mangé une pomme. → Une pomme ....

b. Léonard de Vinci a peint la Joconde. → ....

c. L'oiseau a mangé le ver de terre. → ....

d. Daniel a planté les jonquilles. → ....

e. Mathilde a décoré l'appartement. → ....

8 **Active or passive voice? Tick the correct column.**

	Active	Passive
a. Les cambrioleurs ont été surpris par les policiers.	☐	☐
b. Notre président était respecté de tous.	☐	☐
c. On interdit l'utilisation des téléphones portables dans la salle d'attente.	☐	☐
d. Ce fruit ne se mange pas.	☐	☐
e. Karine est très appréciée de ses collègues.	☐	☐

Verbs with no passive voice

- To be used in the passive voice, verbs must be transitive (used with a direct object). A direct object answers the question *What?* in reference to the action of the verb: **Coralie fait (quoi ?) une tarte. = La tarte a été faite par Coralie.** (**faire** = transitive verb)
- Intransitive verbs cannot be made passive in French. These include verbs that are followed by **à** + **quelqu'un** (indirect object): **apprendre, conseiller, demander, dire, refuser**.
- Verbs that take **être** in the perfect tense cannot be made passive either.

9 Can these verbs be used in the passive voice? Tick YES or NO.

		YES	NO
demander	*quelque chose à quelqu'un*	☐	☐
construire	*quelque chose pour quelqu'un*	☐	☐
aller	*quelque part*	☐	☐
admirer	*par quelqu'un*	☐	☐
promettre	*quelque chose à quelqu'un*	☐	☐
monter	*les escaliers*	☐	☐
manger	*quelque chose*	☐	☐
tomber	*par terre*	☐	☐

Pas mal ! You have reached the end of Lesson 17! It's time to count up the icons for the exercises and record your result here and in the table on page 128.

18

The present subjunctive

The present subjunctive

The subjunctive is a verb form called a grammatical mood. All the tenses we have seen so far have been in the indicative mood, which is used for giving factual information. The subjunctive mood is used to express wish, possibility, opinion, etc.

The present subjunctive
This tense is formed by taking the 3rd-person plural (**ils/elles**) present tense (in the indicative) and replacing the **-ent** ending with the following endings:
-e, -es, -e, -ions, -iez, -ent

regarder	
que je regard	**-e**
que tu regard	**-es**
qu'il/elle regard	**-e**
que nous regard	**-ions**
que vous regard	**-iez**
qu'ils regard	**-ent**

vendre	
que je vend	**-e**
que tu vend	**-es**
qu'il/elle vend	**-e**
que nous vend	**-ions**
que vous vend	**-iez**
qu'ils vend	**-ent**

finir	
que je finiss	**-e**
que tu finiss	**-es**
qu'il/elle finiss	**-e**
que nous finiss	**-ions**
que vous finiss	**-iez**
qu'ils finiss	**-ent**

1 Underline the verb conjugated in the subjunctive.

a. Il faut que je **réussis / réussisse** mon examen pour entrer à l'université.

b. Je dois prendre ma douche avant que Jean **vienne / vient** me chercher !

c. Pourvu que nous **vendons / vendions** la voiture rapidement !

d. Nous sommes très contents que tu **agrandisses / agrandis** la maison !

e. Il est important que tu **prends / prennes** ton passeport si tu veux vraiment prendre ton avion !

2 Change the verbs in the present indicative to the present subjunctive.

a. Je **mange** du popcorn. → Il est étonnant que je .... du popcorn.

b. Tu **écoutes** la radio. → Il est important que tu .... la radio.

c. Elle **maigrit** très vite. → Il est surprenant qu'elle .... très vite.

d. Nous **mettons** la table. → Il est utile que nous .... la table.

e. Vous **perdez** souvent vos affaires. → Il est bizarre que vous .... souvent vos affaires.

f. Ils **choisissent** toujours les bonnes cartes. → Il est étonnant qu'ils .... toujours les bonnes cartes.

être and *avoir*

The verbs **être** and **avoir** are irregular in the present subjunctive:

être		avoir	
que je	**sois**	que j'	**aie**
que tu	**sois**	que tu	**aies**
qu'il	**soit**	qu'il	**ait**
que nous	**soyons**	que nous	**ayons**
que vous	**soyez**	que vous	**ayez**
qu'ils	**soient**	qu'ils	**aient**

3 Complete the sentences with a conjugated form of *être* in the present subjunctive.

a. Il faut que tu .... sur ton trente et un pour le mariage de ta sœur !

b. Il est essentiel que nous .... honnêtes durant cet entretien.

c. Je me suis levée en avance pour que vous .... à l'heure.

d. Il est content que je .... premier de ma classe !

e. Il se peut qu'elle .... coupable de quelques délits.

f. Bien qu'ils .... très occupés, ils ont trouvé le temps de venir.

4 **Complete the sentences with a conjugated form of *avoir* in the present subjunctive.**

a. Bien que je n'.................................... pas beaucoup de temps, je viendrai te voir samedi prochain.

b. Il faut que tu .... de bons résultats à cet examen.

c. Il est impossible qu'elle .... son portefeuille sur elle. Il doit être chez elle !

d. Je suis surpris qu'ils .... un tel courage.

e. Nous sommes désolées que vous .... mal à la tête. Ce doit être la chaleur !

f. Je crains que nous .... de la pluie demain.

Irregular verbs in the subjunctive

- The following verbs are highly irregular:

aller: (que) j'aille, tu ailles, il/elle aille, nous allions, vous alliez, ils/elles aillent

faire: (que) je fasse, tu fasses, il/elle fasse, nous fassions, vous fassiez, ils/elles fassent

pouvoir: (que) je puisse, tu puisses, il/elle puisse, nous puissions, vous puissiez, ils/elles puissent

savoir: (que) je sache, tu saches, il/elle sache, nous sachions, vous sachiez, ils/elles sachent

vouloir: (que) je veuille, tu veuilles, il/elle veuille, nous voulions, vous vouliez, ils/elles veuillent

- In some **-er** verbs, a spelling change occurs in all persons except for the first- and second-person plural (**nous** and **vous**) (see 'Talking about the present', page 55).

- Some verbs have two spelling changes: one that occurs in **nous** and **vous** forms, which take the same stem as the imperfect tense, and one in the other persons:

boire: (que) je boive, tu boives, il/elle boive, nous buvions, vous buviez, ils/elles boivent

devoir: (que) je doive, tu doives, il/elle doive, nous devions, vous deviez, ils/elles doivent

prendre: (que) je prenne, tu prennes, il/elle prenne, nous prenions, vous preniez, ils/elles prennent

recevoir: (que) je reçoive, tu reçoives, il/elle reçoive, nous recevions, vous receviez, ils/elles reçoivent

tenir: (que) je tienne, tu tiennes, il/elle tienne, nous tenions, vous teniez, ils/elles tiennent

venir: (que) je vienne, tu viennes, il/elle vienne, nous venions, vous veniez, ils/elles viennent

5 Complete each sentence with the correct verb.

ailles
fasses
veniez
deviez
saches
prenne

a. Nous sommes heureux que vous .... au restaurant avec nous !

b. Il faut que tu .... que je t'ai toujours dit la vérité.

c. Je voudrais que tu .... la vaisselle ce soir.

d. Il est probable que vous .... passer chez nous avant de partir.

e. Il se peut que ton père .... la voiture ce soir.

f. Il faut que tu .... chez le dentiste.

6 Conjugate these verbs in the present subjunctive.

a. Il est étonnant que vous .... (boire) du vin !

b. Je doute qu'ils .... (aller) en Espagne cette année.

c. Il est possible que tu .... (recevoir) une lettre de tante Agathe.

d. Il faut que tu .... (tenir) la corde de ce côté.

e. J'ai peur que vous .... (faire) la queue pendant longtemps.

The subjunctive after conjunctions

The subjunctive is required after expressions such as:

à condition que *provided that*
afin que *in order that*
à moins que *unless*
avant que *before*
bien que *although*
jusqu'à ce que *until*
pour que *so that*
pourvu que *provided that*
quoique *although*
sans que *without*

7 **Complete the sentences using the appropriate conjunction that requires the subjunctive.**

a. Je viendrai samedi, ... je ne vienne dimanche.

b. Je t'ai apporté cette couverture .... tu n'aies pas froid.

c. .... je n'aime pas le poisson, j'ai plutôt apprécié ce dîner.

d. .... il ne vienne pas avec sa femme. Quelle pimbêche !

e. Je continuerai les leçons .... je comprenne toutes les notions.

BIEN QUE | POUR QUE | JUSQU'À CE QUE | À MOINS QUE | POURVU QUE

The subjunctive after verbs that express wishes, feelings & opinions

The subjunctive is required after these verbs with **que**:

demander que *to ask that*
désirer que *to want that*
espérer que *to hope that*
préférer que *to prefer that*
souhaiter que *to wish that*
vouloir que *to want that*
avoir peur que *to fear that*
craindre que *to fear that*
être content que *to be pleased that*
être désolé que *to be sorry that*
être heureux que *to be happy that*
être surpris que *to be surprised that*
regretter que *to regret that*

8 Conjugate these verbs in the present subjunctive.

a. Je souhaiterais que nous .... (gagner) au loto !

b. Il veut que tu .... (venir) avec ton fiancé.

c. J'ai peur que vous .... (finir) tout le gâteau !

d. Je suis surpris que tu .... (vouloir) retourner dans cet hôtel.

e. Je suis désolé que vous n' .... (avoir) pas de chance aujourd'hui.

The subjunctive after expressions conveying possibility & doubt

The subjunctive is required after:

douter que *to doubt that*
il est douteux que *it is doubtful that*
il est impossible que *it's impossible that*
il est possible que *it's possible that*
il est probable que *it is probable that*
il semble que *it seems that*
il se peut que *it's possible that*

9 Choose the most appropriate expression of possibility or doubt from the list above given each context.

a. .... je perde encore une fois !

b. .... il y ait de l'orage demain. 70 % de probabilité selon le bureau de météorologie.

c. .... nous soyons sélectionnées pour l'équipe nationale ! Cela serait merveilleux !

d. .... ma jambe soit cassée. La radiographie nous en dira plus.

e. .... j'aie la rubéole. Je l'ai eue quand j'étais petit.

The subjunctive after impersonal expressions

The subjunctive is required after expressions such as:

il est bizarre que *it is odd that*

il est bon que *it is good that*

c'est dommage que *it's a pity that*

il est essentiel que *it is essential that*

il est étonnant que *it is surprising that*

il faut que *it is necessary that*

il est important que *it is important that*

il est nécessaire que *it is necessary that*

il est utile que *it is useful that*

il vaut mieux que *it is better that*

10 **Conjugate these verbs preceded by impersonal expressions using *que* in the present subjunctive.**

a. Il serait étonnant que je ....**(recevoir)** une lettre d'Olivier. Cela fait des années que je n'ai pas eu de ses nouvelles.

b. C'est dommage que tu ne ....**(boire)** pas de cidre ! C'est tellement bon !

c. Il vaut mieux que nous ....**(aller)** au cinéma demain : ils annoncent de la pluie.

d. C'est bizarre que tu ....**(avoir)** un chien : je croyais que tu étais allergique !

e. Il faut que nous ....**(rendre)** nos livres à la bibliothèque avant samedi.

More on uses of the subjunctive

- The most frequent use of the subjunctive is in subordinate clauses, usually after the word **que** *that* when there is a change in subject: **Il faut que j'aille.** *It is necessary that I go.*
- So it is often used after superlatives: **C'est le meilleur livre que j'aie jamais lu !** *It's the best book I have ever read!* (Note that the tense used here is the past subjunctive composed of auxiliary **avoir** in the present subjunctive followed by the past participle of the verb **lire**.)
- And after indefinite expressions such as **où que** *wherever*, **qui que** *whoever*, **quoi que** *whatever*, **quel que** *whichever*: **Où que tu sois, je te trouverai !**
- It is also used after verbs of believing and thinking (such as **croire** or **penser**) in the negative: **Je ne pense pas qu'il soit allé au théâtre** (past subjunctive composed of the auxiliary **être** in the present subjunctive followed by the past participle of the verb **aller**).

II Complete these sentences.

a. C'est le meilleur film que j' .... jamais vu !

b. .... tu ailles, je penserai à toi.

c. .... tu fasses, je t'aimerai toujours.

d. Je ne crois pas qu'il .... allé en ville.

e. Je ne pense pas qu'il .... de viande.

Well done! You've reached the end of Lesson 18! It's time to count up the icons for the exercises and record your result here and in the table on page 128.

19

The past historic

The past historic (*Le passé simple*)

- The past historic tense is rarely used in spoken language, but is still employed in formal written French. It is used to describe one-off completed actions in the past. It is most commonly found in historical writing or in storytelling. Today, in everyday speech and journalism, the perfect tense **(passé composé)** is far more common.
- Most verbs are regular in the past historic. This tense is formed by replacing the infinitive ending with the endings below, which differ for the three verb groups:

	-er **verbs** (e.g. **regarder**)	**Most *-ir* verbs** (e.g. **finir**) **Some *-re* or *-oir* verbs**	**Other** (e.g. **vouloir**)
je	**regard -ai**	**fin -is**	**voul -us**
tu	**regard -as**	**fin -is**	**voul -us**
il/elle	**regard -a**	**fin -it**	**voul -ut**
nous	**regard -âmes**	**fin -îmes**	**voul -ûmes**
vous	**regard -âtes**	**fin -îtes**	**voul -ûtes**
ils/elles	**regard -èrent**	**fin -irent**	**voul -urent**

1 **Underline all the verbs in the past historic tense in this story.**

Il était une fois un meunier qui, lorsqu'il mourut, légua tous ses biens à ses trois fils. L'aîné hérita d'un moulin, le cadet d'un âne, et le plus jeune, Paul, d'un chat. « Lorsque je l'aurai mangé, soupira-t-il, il ne me restera plus qu'à mourir de faim ! » Mais le chat l'entendit et prépara un plan : « Ne me mangez pas, Maître. Si vous me laissez en vie, je vous apporterai tout ce que vous désirez. » Paul était sceptique, mais fit ce que le chat lui demandait : « Aussi, si quelqu'un vous le demande, vous vous appelez désormais monsieur le Marquis de Carabas », ajouta le chat.
Le chat mit de la nourriture dans son sac et s'allongea sur le sol, comme mort.

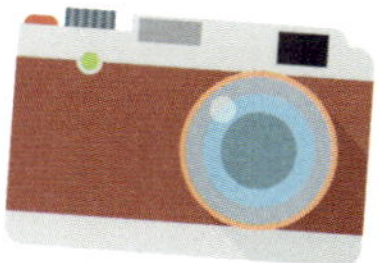

2 Conjugate these verbs in the historic past.

a. La réunion .... (débuter) à 10 heures.

b. Clément et Zoé .... (arriver) à l'aéroport à l'heure.

c. Nous .... (attendre) pendant des heures. La tension .... (monter).

d. Vous .... (partir). La maison .... (sembler) vide.

e. Je .... (prendre) beaucoup de photos ce jour-là.

avoir and *être*

These verbs are irregular in the historic past:

avoir
j'eus
tu eus
il/elle eut
nous eûmes
vous eûtes
ils/elles eurent

être
je fus
tu fus
il/elle fut
nous fûmes
vous fûtes
ils/elles furent

3 Complete the sentences with the correct form of *avoir* conjugated in the past historic.

a. Elles .... soudain très soif.

b. Nous .... l'idée d'aller au cinéma tous ensemble.

c. Lorsqu'elle ouvrit la fenêtre, j'.................... très froid.

d. Il .... une peur bleue lorsque la foudre tomba sur la maison voisine !

e. Ils .... beaucoup de difficultés à organiser ce voyage.

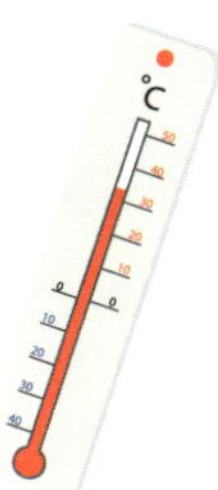

4 **Complete the sentences with the correct form of *être* conjugated in the past historic.**

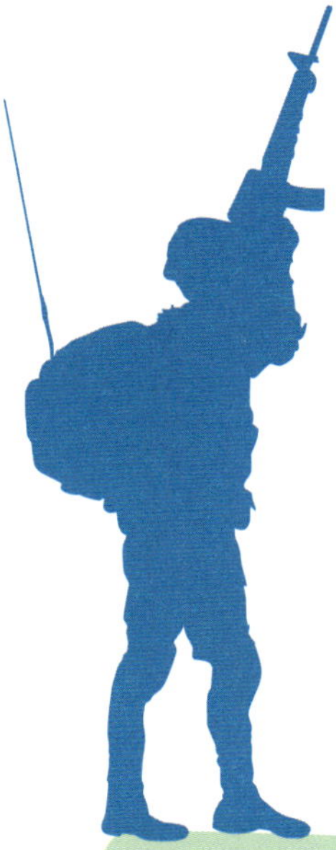

a. Ils .... les premiers soldats américains à Paris.

b. Nous .... très surpris.

c. Louis de Funès .... très célèbre dans les années 1970.

d. Tu .... un des élèves les plus populaires du lycée !

e. Vous .... très heureux de réussir votre examen.

Irregular verbs

All **-oir** verbs are irregular in the past historic. Here are some other irregular verbs:

aller: j'allai, tu allas, il/elle alla, nous allâmes, vous allâtes, ils/elles allèrent

boire: je bus, tu bus, il/elle but, nous bûmes, vous bûtes, ils/elles burent

connaître: je connus, tu connus, il/elle connut, nous connûmes, vous connûtes, ils/elles connurent

courir:je courus, tu courus, il/elle courut, nous courûmes, vous courûtes, ils/elles coururent

croire: je crus, tu crus, il/elle crut, nous crûmes, vous crûtes, ils/elles crurent

devoir: je dus, tu dus, il/elle dut, nous dûmes, vous dûtes, ils/elles durent

dire: je dis, tu dis, il/elle dit, nous dîmes, vous dîtes, ils/elles dirent

écrire: j'écrivis, tu écrivis, il/elle écrivit, nous écrivîmes, vous écrivîtes, ils/elles écrivirent

faire: je fis, tu fis, il/elle fit, nous fîmes, vous fîtes, ils/elles firent

falloir: il fallut

mettre: je mis, tu mis, il/elle mit, nous mîmes, vous mîtes, ils/elles mirent

prendre: je pris, tu pris, il/elle prit, nous prîmes, vous prîtes, ils/elles prirent

savoir: je sus, tu sus, il/elle sut, nous sûmes, vous sûtes, ils/elles surent

tenir: je tins, tu tins, il/elle tint, nous tînmes, vous tîntes, ils/elles tinrent

venir: je vins, tu vins, il/elle vint, nous vînmes, vous vîntes, ils/elles vinrent

voir: je vis, tu vis, il/elle vit, nous vîmes, vous vîtes, ils/elles virent

5 Underline the irregular past historic verbs in the following story.

Le Petit Poucet dut se lever de bon matin et prit le chemin du ruisseau. Il emplit ses poches de petits cailloux blancs et revint ensuite à la maison. Il alla dans une forêt dense. Le bûcheron se mit à couper du bois et les enfants ramassèrent des brindilles. Lorsque les parents virent que les enfants étaient occupés, ils s'enfuirent rapidement. Le Petit Poucet courut partout pour retrouver ses parents mais dut renoncer, tristement.

6 Conjugate the following irregular verbs in the past historic tense.

a. Elle .... **(mettre)** sa robe rapidement pour ne pas être en retard !

b. Ils .... **(reconnaître)** le bandit et lui .... **(courir)** après.

c. Je .... **(savoir)** immédiatement que quelque chose lui était arrivé.

d. Nous .... **(aller)** au restaurant après la cérémonie.

e. Tu .... **(être obligée de)** prendre le train plus tard que prévu suite aux intempéries.

Verbs ending in *-ger* and *-cer*

- In the past historic, verbs ending in **-ger** or **-cer** undergo a spelling change to retain the same pronunciation: **-g** changes to **-ge** and **-c** changes to **-ç**.
- This spelling change occurs in all persons except the third-person plural.

manger: je man**ge**ai, tu man**ge**as, il/elle man**ge**a, nous man**ge**âmes, vous man**ge**âtes, ils/elles mangèrent

lancer: je lan**ç**ai, tu lan**ç**as, il/elle lan**ç**a, nous lan**ç**âmes, vous lan**ç**âtes, ils/elles lancèrent

7 Conjugate these verbs in the past historic tense.

a. Ils .... (avancer) dans la neige avec difficulté.

b. Nous .... (voyager) pendant deux mois !

c. Il .... (neiger) toute la journée et toute la nuit sans interruption.

d. Vous .... (commencer) la réunion sans Romain, qui était en retard.

e. Martin .... (remplacer) David qui était malade.

f. Vous .... (nager) pendant deux heures : quelles athlètes !

8 Complete the crossword by conjugating these regular and irregular verbs in the past historic.

Down

1. j'............... **(habiller)**
2. nous .... **(tenir)**
3. ils .... **(finir)**
4. elle .... **(remplacer)**

Across

5. il .... **(hurler)**
6. nous .... **(boire)**
7. il .... **(falloir)**
8. elle .... **(regarder)**
9. elles .... **(placer)**

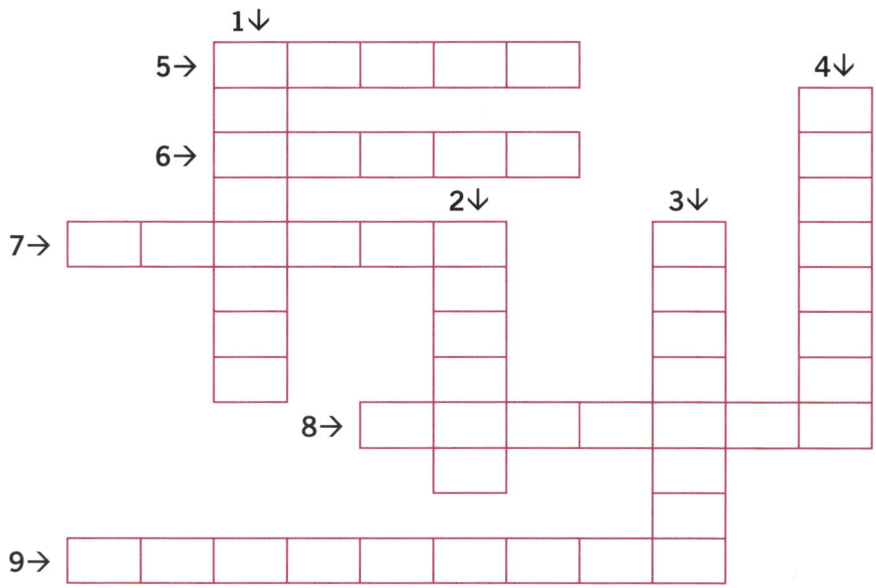

9 ***La petite poule rousse*: fill in the missing words in the story with the appropriate verbs in the past historic.**

Il était une fois une petite poule rousse qui .... de chez elle pour aller en ville. Elle .... la clé dans sa poche mais sa poche avait un trou et la clé .... par terre. La petite poule ne le .... pas et .... son chemin. Maître Renard .... Il n'avait qu'une envie : manger la poulette ! Lorsqu'il .... la clé sur le sol, il la .... et .... ouvrir la porte de la maisonnette.

apparut | sortit | aperçut | vit | courut | poursuivit | mit | ramassa | tomba

Excellent ! You've reached the end of Lesson 19! It's time to count up the icons for the exercises and record your result here and in the table on page 128.

20
Review

1 Fill in the appropriate definite or indefinite article (i.e. the equivalent of *the* or *a/an*) in the following French expressions.

a. J'ai .... cafard. (masc.)
➜ *literally, 'I have the cockroach.' = I feel down.*

b. Tu me casses .... oreilles !
➜ *lit. 'You are breaking my ears.' = The noise you are making is really irritating me.*

c. Il m'a posé .... lapin !
➜ *lit. 'He put me down a rabbit.' = He stood me up.*

d. C'est .... fin .... haricots !
➜ *lit. 'It is the end of the beans.' = It's the last straw.*

e. Arrête de faire .... andouille ! (type of sausage)
➜ *lit. 'Stop making the sausage.' = Stop acting like a fool!*

2 Unscramble the following occupations and then translate them into English.

a. preesfousr = un ....

b. canuhetr = un ....

c. veesudne = une ....

d. méecdin = un ....

e. iégienunr = un ....

f. seuvrer = un ....

g. cceiogrne = un ....

h. blugeonar = un ....

3 Underline the odd one out in each series of words.

a. as – est – avez – ont – ai

b. mangé – choisi – fait – étant – porté

c. te – lui – me – je – leur

d. Français – Mexique – Australien – Hollandais – Italien

e. bleu – rouge – vert – chat – rose

4 Fill in the crossword with the adjectives that correspond to the definitions.

Down
1. Ils sont généreux, prévenants, attentionnés.
2. Contraire de maigre.
3. Il n'arrête pas de parler.
4. Il est beau, mignon.
5. Elle a du chagrin ; elle a envie de pleurer.
6. Il ne rit pas et a l'air grave.
7. La Tour Eiffel est ... (de grande taille).

Across
8. Elles sont réelles, exactes.
9. Contraire de mauvaise.
10. Qui peut attendre ; persévérant.
11. Contraire de petit.
12. Il est âgé.
13. Certain ou sécurisé.
14. Il cherche à faire du mal.

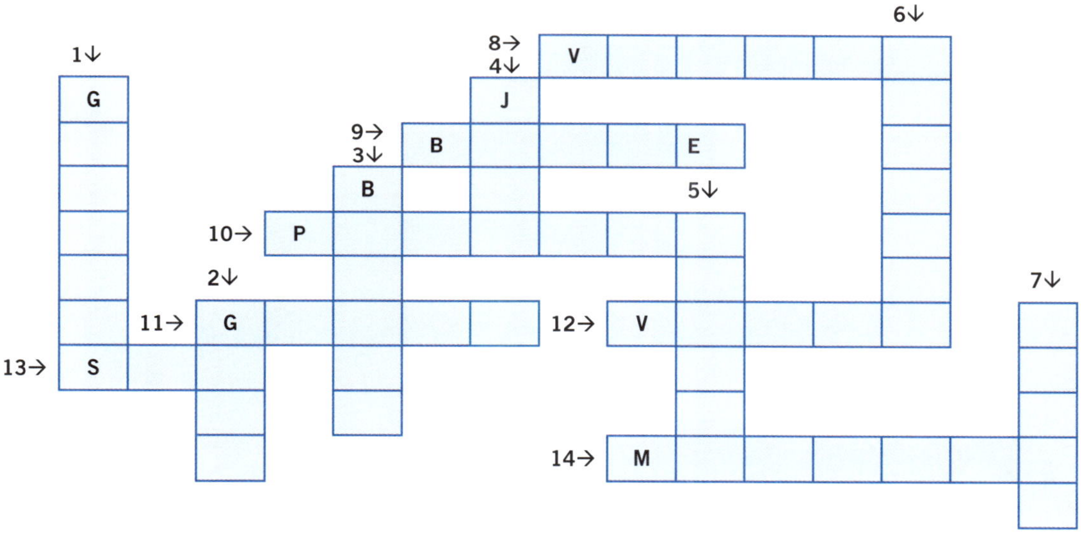

5 Unscramble the words to form sentences.

a. allé / avec / Quentin / amis / est / cinéma / au / ses

....

b. l' / grand / faire / Je / un / pense / prochaine / voyage / année

....

c. une / Ils / pour / anniversaire / organiseront / Marion / fête / d'

....

d. lorsque / faisais / porte / la / la / as / à / Je / sieste / frappé / tu

....

e. dès / travail / commencera / Eva / retour / le / son

....

6 Fill in the table with the conjugations of these regular and irregular verbs in the tenses indicated.

	Present	Perfect	Future	Conditional	Imperfect
regarder	je regarde	j'	je regarderai	je	je ....
faire	tu	tu	tu feras	tu	tu faisais
vendre	il vend	il	il	il vendrait	il ....
finir	nous	nous avons fini	nous finirons	nous	nous ....
boire	vous	vous	vous boirez	vous	vous buviez
aller	elles vont	elles	elles	elles iraient	elles ....

7 Match each clock with the correct time written in words.

01:30
12:00
02:15

Il est une heure trente.
Il est quatre heures et demie.
Il est onze heures moins le quart.
Il est deux heures et quart.
Il est midi.
Il est huit heures moins dix.
Il est trois heures vingt-cinq.

10:45
04:30
07:50
03:25

8 Find these linking words in the grid.

ainsi
néanmoins
pourtant
mais
aussi
car
donc
quand
quoique
lorsque
comme
toutefois

R	E	H	A	C	O	M	M	E	P
G	A	T	I	S	S	O	N	L	O
A	B	O	N	N	U	G	M	O	U
Q	Y	N	S	A	C	I	O	R	R
B	U	K	I	U	J	A	V	S	T
G	Q	O	X	D	Q	F	R	Q	A
M	U	S	I	R	O	I	L	U	N
O	A	B	M	Q	C	N	A	E	T
M	N	X	B	E	U	O	C	Q	L
A	D	O	L	G	F	E	R	A	I
I	T	O	U	T	E	F	O	I	S
S	R	D	J	A	U	S	S	I	A
N	E	A	N	M	O	I	N	S	O

9 Make sentences using the appropriate element from each column.

E.g. Elles	as compris	au cinéma hier.
a. J'	a été	ma tarte aux pommes ?
b. Il	sommes partis	toute la nuit !
c. Vous	ai rêvé	à 8 heures.
d. Tu	avez aimé	l'exercice de grammaire ?
e. Nous	ont dansé	que je gagnais au loto !

E.g. Elles ont dansé toute la nuit !

a. ....

b. ....

c. ....

d. ....

e. ....

10 Match each figure to the corresponding number written in words.

1. 46 •   • **a.** cent cinquante-deux
2. 99 •   • **b.** cinq cent deux
3. 318 •   • **c.** quarante-six
4. 72 •   • **d.** six cent quatre-vingt-trois
5. 502 •   • **e.** mille huit
6. 152 •   • **f.** trois cent dix-huit
7. 1008 •   • **g.** soixante-douze
8. 683 •   • **h.** quatre-vingt-dix-neuf

Félicitations ! You've now completed all the exercises in this workbook! It's time to count up the icons for this section and record your result here and in the final table on page 128.

ANSWERS

1. Alphabet and pronunciation

2 **a.** une mère *a mother* **b.** peut-être *maybe* **c.** Noël *Christmas* **d.** une leçon *a lesson* **e.** le présent *the present* **f.** tôt *early* **g.** un garçon *a boy* **h.** le passé *the past*

3 **a.** père **b.** Noël **c.** glaçons **d.** passé **e.** même

4 froid *cold* – porc *pork* – trois *three* – vous *you* (formal, plural) – abricot *apricot* – chez *at* – mot *word* – chat *cat* – salut *hi* – outil *tool* – estomac *stomach* – beaucoup *a lot, much, many* – trop *too (much/many)* – nerf *nerve* – deux *two*

5 **Silent final letter:** poule – lourd – froid
Voiced final letter: Turc – œuf – four – ours – hiver

7

Sentence	Y	N
un homme	✓	
les élèves	✓	
les haricots		✓
les vieux éléphants	✓	
le petit ami	✓	
les yeux	✓	

8

	1	2	3	4	5	6	7	8	9	10
A					M			H		
B	V			B	O	N	J	O	U	R
C	O			E	T			M		A
D	U			A				M		V
E	S	A	L	U	T			E		I
F				C						E
G		F	R	O	I	D		M		
H				U		E	L	E	V	E
I	T	R	O	P		U		R		
J						X		E		

9 « Mon **père** est **rentré** hier soir du Venezuela pour **fêter Noël** en famille. Il veut des **festivités françaises** ! C'est **génial d'être** enfin ensemble ! C'est l'heure des cadeaux et des escargots ! Nous allons nous **régaler** ! Quelle **fête** cela sera ! »

2. Articles and nouns

1

Nouns	M	F	P
salon	✓		
chambre		✓	
toilettes			✓
cave		✓	
grenier	✓		
cuisine		✓	

2

Masc. singular	Fem. singular	Masc. plural
un ami	une amie	**des amis**
un Français	**une Française**	**des Français**
un marchand	**une marchande**	des marchands
un marié	**une mariée**	**des mariés**
un avocat	une avocate	**des avocats**
un invité	**une invitée**	des invités

3 **a. La** maison est grande ! **b. Les** filles sont très jolies ! **c. Les** enfants sont gentils. **d. L'**eau est trop froide ! **e. Le** garçon joue au football. **f. L'**homme est très grand !

4 le garçon – la chambre – l'araignée – les chaussures – le vent

5 **a.** Il y a **un** chat sur le toit. **b.** As-tu **des** crayons dans ta trousse ? **c.** Je mange **des** gâteaux tous les jours. **d.** Il veut **une** guitare pour Noël. **e.** Nous avons **un** chien.

6 « Garçon, s'il vous plaît ! Je voudrais **une** pizza avec **des** champignons, **du** jambon et **de la** sauce tomate. Je veux **la** pizza rapidement car j'ai très faim ! J'aimerais aussi **de l'**eau ! Merci ! »

7 **a.** Tu **n'**as **pas** de jardin. **b.** Nous **n'**avons **pas** d'enfants. **c.** Ils **n'**ont **pas** de gentils parents. **d.** Je **n'**ai **pas** de maison. **e.** Elles **n'**ont **pas** d'amis.

8 un avocat *a lawyer* – un chanteur *a singer* – un professeur *a teacher* – un serveur *a waiter* – un concierge *a caretaker* – un écrivain *a writer* – un ingénieur *an engineer*

9

Masculine	Feminine
un vendeur	**une vendeuse**
un musicien	une musicienne
un acteur	**une actrice**
un boulanger	une boulangère
un étudiant	une étudiante
un maître	**une maîtresse**
un paysan	**une paysanne**
un secrétaire	une secrétaire
un dentiste	**une dentiste**
un professeur	**une professeure/un professeur**

3. Pronouns

1 **a. Tu** es très grande ! **b. Elle** a quarante-cinq ans. **c. Nous** sommes canadiens. **d. Elles** adorent les araignées ! **e. Vous** êtes très élégantes !

2 **a. Elles** sont au Kenya. **b. Vous** êtes au cinéma ? **c. Elle** est heureuse. **d. Nous** sommes à la boulangerie. **e. Je** suis allergique au pollen.

3 **a.** Il **est** peintre. **b.** Nous **sommes** étudiants. **c.** Elles **sont** actrices. **d.** Vous **êtes** boulangers ? **e.** Je **suis** traducteur.

4 **a.** J'**ai** 45 ans. **b.** Nous **avons** un chien. **c.** Ils **ont** 3 vélos. **d.** Tu **as** une moto ? **e.** Elle **a** 2 maisons.

5 **a.** Philippe **est** ingénieur. **b.** Karine **a** un chien et deux hamsters. **c.** Clémentine **est** très jolie. **d.** Nicolas **est** gentil. **e.** Oriane **a** une belle robe.

6 **a. Elle** est courageuse. **b. Vous** avez une belle voiture ! **c. Nous** sommes en Australie. **d. Ils** sont petits. **e. Je** suis belge.

7 **a.** Je **l'**aime ! **b.** Tu **m'**attends quelques minutes ? **c.** Elles **nous** ont invités au restaurant. **d.** Je **vous** ai vus au cinéma. **e.** Stéphanie **t'**attend depuis une heure.

8 **a.** le train **b.** Maéva ou Bruno **c.** la fourchette **d.** ses cousins ou ses cousines **e.** toi et ton amie

9 **a.** Il **lui** a dit bonjour. **b.** Je **vous** ai donné une lettre. **c.** Marie **nous** pose une question. **d.** Elle **lui** téléphone tous les dimanches. **e.** Ton père **t'**a répondu.

10

						5	
					6	L	A
				3		E	
			4	N	O	U	S
			1	O		R	
	8	7	L	U	I		
2	V	O	U	S			
	O		I				
	U						
	S						

4. Adjectives

1

Masc. sing.	Fem. sing.	Masc. pl.	Fem. pl.
français	française	**français**	françaises
mexicain	mexicaine	mexicains	mexicaines
grand	grande	grands	**grandes**
gros	grosse	**gros**	grosses
poli	**polie**	polis	polies
beau	belle	beaux	**belles**
bon	**bonne**	bons	bonnes
vieux	vieille	vieux	vieilles

2 **a.** Elle est vraiment très **gentille** ! **b.** Ces chiens sont **méchants**. **c.** Sois **patient** Sébastien. **d.** Elles sont vraiment **bavardes** ! **e.** Oh Marceau, avec un tel sourire, toi, tu es **amoureux** ! **f.** Ils sont tellement **maladroits** !

3 **a.** Oh, regarde ! Quel **beau** paysage ! **b.** J'aime beaucoup cette robe **rouge**. **c.** C'est une fille **jalouse**. **d.** Quel **joli** tableau ! **e.** C'était un **long** voyage.

4 **a.** Mon ami est **anglais**. **b.** Cette fille est **coréenne**. **c.** Ses parents sont **finlandais**. **d.** Ce groupe de musique est **canadien**. **e.** Les joueurs de cette équipe sont **chinois**. **f.** Les chanteuses de cette chorale sont **américaines**.

5

Flags	Masc. sing.	Fem. sing.	Masc. pl.	Fem. pl.
	Hollandais	Hollandaise	Hollandais	Hollandaises
	Espagnol	Espagnole	Espagnols	Espagnoles
	Italien	Italienne	Italiens	Italiennes
	Suédois	Suédoise	Suédois	Suédoises
	Irlandais	Irlandaise	Irlandais	Irlandaises
	Norvégien	Norvégienne	Norvégiens	Norvégiennes
	Japonais	Japonaise	Japonais	Japonaises
	Mexicain	Mexicaine	Mexicains	Mexicaines
	Brésilien	Brésilienne	Brésiliens	Brésiliennes
	Allemand	Allemande	Allemands	Allemandes

6

Colours	Masc. sing.	Fem. sing.	Masc. pl.	Fem. pl.
	violet	violette	violets	violettes
	vert	verte	verts	vertes
	bleu	bleue	bleus	bleues
	orange	orange	orange	orange
	gris	grise	gris	grises
	blanc	blanche	blancs	blanches
	noir	noire	noirs	noires
	rouge	rouge	rouges	rouges
	marron	marron	marron	marron
	rose	rose	roses	roses

7 **a.** De belles chaussures **bleues**. **b.** De très jolies fleurs **jaunes**. **c.** De beaux pulls **marron**. **d.** Une élégante cravate **noire**. **e.** Un buisson **vert.**

8 **a.** J'ai beaucoup aimé **ce** film ! **b.** Quelle horreur ! **Cette** pomme était pourrie ! **c. Ces** enfants sont très bruyants. **d.** Peux-tu me passer **ce** plat, s'il te plaît ? **e. Cet** homme a une cravate rigolote !

9 **a.** As-tu vu **mon** livre ? Je ne le trouve pas ! **b. Ses** sœurs sont très grandes ! **c.** J'adore **leur** chien ! Il est très amusant ! **d. Son** amie s'appelle Éléanore. **e. Ton** père est très gentil, Anne !

10 **a.** Il a des cheveux bruns/marron. **b.** Son père est français. **c.** Leur chat est blanc. **d.** Elle s'est lavé les cheveux hier. **e.** Votre maison est très grande !

5. Comparatives and superlatives

1 **a.** Son chat est **moins rapide que** son chien ! **b.** Floriane est **aussi jolie que** Martine. **c.** Ce livre est **plus intéressant que** celui-là. **e.** Laurent est **moins gentil que** Sylvain. **f.** Ta maison est **aussi grande que** la mienne.

2 **a.** This table is bigger than that one. **b.** Alexandre is as sporty as Julien. **c.** Sophie is less pretty than Karine. **d.** Julien is as funny as Lily. **e.** The blue bag is bigger than the black one.

3 **a.** Elles sont plus **bavardes** que nous. **b.** Marion est aussi **belle** que Sophie. **c.** Mathieu est aussi **intelligent** que Claire. **d.** Louis et Gabriel sont moins **gentils** que Catherine et Jennifer. **e.** L'arbre de droite est plus **petit** que l'arbre de gauche.

4 **Adjectives:** gentil – belle **Adverbs:** rapidement – mieux – facilement – malheureusement

5 **a.** rare > **rarement** **b.** poli > **poliment** **c.** courageux > **courageuse** > **courageusement** **d.** prudent > **prudemment** **e.** parfait > **parfaite** > **parfaitement**

6 **a.** C'est **la** plus belle maison du quartier. **b.** Ce sont les garçons **les** plus polis de la classe ! **c.** Ce sont **les** robes les plus laides du magasin. **d.** C'est **le** chien le plus méchant du quartier. **e.** C'est **la** fille la plus jolie du village.

7 **a.** Ces fleurs sont les plus **colorées** du jardin. **b.** Elle est la plus **active** de sa classe. **c.** Ce bébé est le plus **mignon** que je connaisse. **d.** Leurs voitures sont les plus **propres** de la rue ! **e.** Jeanne est la femme la plus **maladroite** que je connaisse !

8 **a.** C'est la maison **la** plus chère du quartier. **b.** Sophie est la fille **la** moins sportive du groupe. **c.** Jonathan est le garçon le plus rapide **de** son club. **d.** Les dattes sont les fruits **les** plus sucrés. **e.** Joséphine est la plus maligne **de** l'école.

9 **a.** Élisa est **aussi étourdie que** Vanessa. **b.** C'est **le meilleur** gâteau du menu. **c.** Ils sont **plus timides que** leurs parents. **d.** Audrey est la fille **la plus généreuse que** je connaisse. **e.** Ce livre est **le pire que** j'aie jamais lu !

6. Sentences and word order

1	Subject	Verb	Complement
a.	Il	mange	du gâteau.
b.	Nous	avons vu	Charles et Simon.
c.	Vous	chantez	une belle mélodie.
d.	Elle	donne	des bonbons.
e.	Nous	aimons	les films de science-fiction.

2 **a.** Julie a invité ses amis au restaurant. **b.** Sylvain a acheté une nouvelle voiture. **c.** Son pull est très joli. **d.** Christian voyage souvent en train. **e.** Léon prend son petit déjeuner à 8 heures.

3 **a.** Estelle **n'est plus** malade. **b.** Martine **n'a ni** chat **ni** chien. **c.** Stéphanie **n'est pas** méchante. **d.** Roger **n'a jamais** mangé de calamar. **e.** Julian **n'a rien** bu hier soir.

4 **a.** Achille **n'aime pas** les fraises. **b.** Violette **ne** joue **pas / jamais** au tennis. **c.** Romain **n'est pas** blond. **d.** Séverine **n'aime pas** les films d'aventure. **e.** Olivier **n'est pas** petit.

5 **a.** Est-ce que Ginette aime les poires ? **b.** Françoise parle-t-elle le chinois ? **c.** Est-ce que Marine vit en Australie ? **d.** Peut-il venir me voir ? **e.** Veut-elle écouter mon CD ?

6 **a.** Est-ce qu'il déteste les chats ? **b.** Est-ce que tu vas au cinéma ? **c.** Est-ce que vous regardez la télé ? **d.** Est-ce qu'ils sont allés en Italie ? **e.** Est-ce qu'elle aime ma confiture ?

7 **a.** **À quelle heure** son train arrive-t-il à la gare ? **b.** **Qui** a mangé mon yaourt ? **c.** **Combien** ce collier coûte-t-il ? **d.** **Comment** es-tu rentré ? **e.** **Que** fait-il dans sa chambre ?

8 **a.** Comment vas-tu ? / Comment allez-vous ? **b.** Où habite-t-il ? **c.** Combien de temps le film a-t-il duré ? **d.** Pourquoi Sophie est-elle rentrée ? **e.** Qui a cassé le vase ?

9 **a.** Je ne vais jamais au théâtre. **b.** Qui a pris mon livre ? **c.** Quand rentre-t-elle ? **d.** Je préfère le pantalon bleu. **e.** Il ne veut pas sortir ce soir.

10 « Allô, Louise ? **Où** es-tu ? Nous sommes inquiets. Nous **ne** savons **pas** où tu es. **Qu'est-ce que** tu fais ? **Pourquoi** n'as-tu pas téléphoné ? **Ne** recommence **jamais** ! »

7. More on pronouns

1 **a.** Elle **se** réveille à 7 heures tous les matins. **b.** Je **me** souviens de Bruno. **c.** Nous **nous** sommes encore disputés. **d.** Vous **vous** téléphonez souvent ? **e.** Il ne **s'**est pas rasé ce matin.

2 **a.** Elle **se lève** très tôt le mardi matin. **b.** Je **m'habille** toujours en jean ! **c.** Il ne **se lave** jamais. Quelle horreur ! **d.** Nous **nous amusons** beaucoup ! Vive les vacances ! **e.** Vous **vous couchez** à quelle heure le samedi soir ?

3 **les montres** = celles – **l'enfant** = celui – **la chambre** = celle – **les jupes** = celles – **le manteau** = celui – **les livres** = ceux

4 **a.** celui-ci **b.** celle-ci **c.** ceux-là **d.** celui-là **e.** ceux-ci

5 **a.** **Que** fais-tu dans la cuisine ? **b.** **Qui** a pris mon manteau ? **c.** **Que** veut-il faire ce soir ? **d.** **Qui** est ce jeune homme ? **e.** **Qui** a apporté le gâteau ?

6 « **Quelle** robe veux-tu mettre aujourd'hui ? – Je ne sais pas. Celle qui est jolie. – **Laquelle** ? – La bleue. – Et **quelles** chaussures veux-tu porter ? – Celles qui sont confortables. Mais **lesquelles** ? – Les sandales. Et **quel** chapeau aimerais-tu ? Celui avec une fleur. Merci ! » **[lequel]** n'est pas utilisé.

7 **a.** J'aime **la leur**. **b.** J'aime **le sien**. **c.** J'aime **les nôtres**. **d.** J'aime **la tienne**. **e.** J'aime **les siennes**.

8 **a.** L'enfant **qui** pleurait était perdu. **b.** Le dernier film **que** j'ai vu était merveilleux. **c.** La tarte **que** maman a préparée est délicieuse ! **d.** Je connais la femme **qui** est devant la boutique. **e.** Je déteste le parfum **que** tu portes aujourd'hui.

9 **a.** Le bébé a pleuré toute la nuit, **ce que** j'ai trouvé fatigant. **b.** Il pleut encore, **ce qui** est très ennuyeux. **c.** Je t'ai dit de ranger ta chambre, **ce que** je t'ai déjà demandé 3 fois ! **d.** Le professeur est absent, **ce qui** signifie que nous pouvons rentrer chez nous. **e.** Il a amené des fleurs, **ce que** je trouve très gentil.

10 **a.** As-tu des livres? Oui j'**en** ai. **b.** Est-il passé au bureau ? Oui, il **y** est allé. **c.** As-tu acheté des poires ? Non, je n'**en** ai pas acheté. **d.** Avons-nous des stylos noirs ? Oui, nous **en** avons. **e.** Jacques était-il au magasin ? Non, il n'**y** était pas.

8. Numbers and time

1 8 **huit** – 14 **quatorze** – 21 **vingt et un** – 50 **cinquante** – 70 **soixante-dix** – 76 **soixante-seize** – 80 **quatre-vingts** – 90 **quatre-vingt-dix** – 200 **deux cents** – 2 000 **deux mille**

2 2 + 5 = **sept** – 10 x 8 = **quatre-vingts** – 9 x 2 = **dix-huit** – 10 000 ÷ 10 = **mille** – 51 + 22 = **soixante-treize** – 30 – 9 = **vingt et un** – 35 + 39 = **soixante-quatorze** – 216 ÷ 6 = **trente-six**

3 Number 11 (**onze**) is different: it is the only odd number. All the others are even numbers!

4 4ᵉ = **quatrième** – 9ᵉ = **neuvième** – 16ᵉ = **seizième** – 17ᵉ = **dix-septième** – 21ᵉ = **vingt et unième** – 26ᵉ = **vingt-sixième** – 1 000ᵉ = **millième**

5 **a.** quarantième **b.** cent vingt-neuvième **c.** premier **d.** soixantième **e.** millième **f.** trentième

6 mardi – jeudi – samedi – dimanche

7 février – avril – juin – août – octobre – décembre

8 **a.** I saw Jean-Philippe the day before yesterday. **b.** What did you do the day after? **c.** Do you want to go to the cinema next Friday? **d.** Ella saw this movie last Tuesday. **e.** The weather is really beautiful today!

9 **a.** treize heures quinze / et quart **b.** seize heures trente **c.** quatre heures quarante-cinq / cinq heures moins le quart **d.** vingt heures quarante **e.** dix heures vingt-cinq

10 Lundi à **neuf heures** M. Dupouy doit se rendre à une réunion qui a lieu au bureau. À **midi et demi** il déjeune avec M. Gosseaume à la Brasserie Dijonnaise puis à **quatorze heures dix** il participe à la présentation du nouveau produit de la compagnie. Le soir même à **dix-huit heures vingt-cinq** il prend l'avion pour Paris.

Le lendemain, M. Dupouy a un rendez-vous avec Dr Garrant à **neuf heures trente**, suivi d'une réunion à La Défense à **onze heures**. Il doit déjeuner à Montmartre à **midi vingt** avec son ami Bastian puis se rend à l'aéroport pour son vol de **quatorze heures quinze**. Il dîne avec sa femme, Marie à **dix-neuf heures**.

Le mercredi, M. Dupouy a un déjeuner avec un collaborateur à **huit heures vingt** puis doit se rendre à une conférence à **treize heures quarante-cinq** à Dijon. À **dix-huit heures**, il doit aller à l'école de son fils pour rencontrer l'instituteur.

11 **a.** 90 € **b.** 6 pièces de 50 cents **c.** 3 lapins et 2 poules **d.** 800 minutes (13 heures et 30 minutes)

9. Verbs & the perfect tense

1 **a.** manger **b.** boire **c.** aller **d.** dormir **e.** vouloir

2

	1st group	2nd group	3rd group
chanter	✓		
punir		✓	
rendre			✓
écouter	✓		
pleuvoir			✓
grandir		✓	
devenir			✓
danser	✓		
apprendre			✓

3 **a. détester > détesté b. dîner > dîné c. aimer > aimé d. écouter > écouté e. perdre > perdu f. prendre > pris**

4 **a.** Hier, nous avons **appris** une nouvelle leçon ! **b.** Il m'a **offert** un magnifique bouquet de roses ! **c.** Elle a **voulu** rentrer tôt à la maison. **d.** Nous avons **pu** rencontrer le chanteur du groupe. **e.** Vous avez **fait** vos devoirs ?

5 **a.** Elles ont **lu** tous les livres. **b.** Elles les ont tous **lus**. **c.** Nous avons **copié** toutes les pages. **d.** Nous les avons toutes **copiées**. **e.** Elle n'a pas **pleuré** longtemps.

6 **a.** Elle est **allée** en ville avec Sonia. **b.** Clarèle et moi sommes **rentrés** (moi=m.) / **rentrées** (moi=f.). **c.** Éléanore et Audrey sont **parties** après le film. **d.** Alain n'est pas **arrivé**. **e.** Jean-Luc et Jérôme sont **venus** à 18 heures.

7 **a.** Ils se sont encore **disputés** ! **b.** Elles se sont **échangé** leurs adresses. **c.** Elle s'est **coupé** le doigt. **d.** Elles se sont **endormies** devant la télé. **e.** Ils se sont **regardés** pendant de longues minutes.

8 **1.c.** J'ai gagné la course ! **2.a.** Nous avons vu ta sœur ce matin. **3.e.** Tu es rentrée à quelle heure ? **4.f.** Elles sont allées au marché ce matin. **5.d.** Vous êtes restés au parc toute la journée ? **6.b.** Ils ont rangé leur chambre.

9 **a.** Nous avons **regardé** la télévision toute la nuit ! **b.** Elles sont **entrées** par la porte de secours. **c.** J'ai **mis** la voiture dans le garage. **d.** Tu as **vu** l'éclipse hier soir ? **e.** Samuel et Laurence ont **écouté** la radio pendant deux heures ! **f.** Nous avons **pris** un taxi pour rentrer.

10 **2.e.** Elles ont téléphoné à l'hôtel pour réserver une chambre. **3.d.** Elles ont déposé leurs bagages dans la chambre. **4.f.** Elles ont demandé au concierge l'adresse d'un bon restaurant. **5.a.** Elles sont restées deux heures au restaurant. **6.c.** Elles sont rentrées à l'hôtel se coucher.

10. Talking about the present

1 **a. Tu** marches vite. **b. Elles** chantent sous la pluie. **c. Je** porte des chaussures. **d. Nous** aidons les sans-abri. **e. Vous** dansez très bien ! **f. Je** pense trop !

2 **a.** Les touristes **visitent** le musée. **b.** Tu **portes** une jolie jupe. **c.** Nous **aimons** la musique classique. **d.** À quelle heure **arrivez**-vous ? **e.** Il **chante** très bien.

3 **a.** Je **travaille** dans l'informatique. **b.** Tu **visites** ce musée souvent ? **c.** Il **débute** le travail à 10 heures. **d.** Nous **dessinons** ce château régulièrement. **e.** Vous ne **montez** pas les escaliers ? **f.** Elles **parlent** trop vite !

4 **a.** Nous **achetons** des pizzas tous les samedis. **b.** Qui **appellent**-ils ? **c.** Il **jette** ses vieilles chaussures. **d.** Vous **espérez** encore voir Brad Pitt ! **e.** Nous **envoyons** la lettre.

5 **a.** Nous **commençons** la réunion à 10 heures. **b.** Je **préfère** le pain complet. **c.** Nous **mangeons** au restaurant ce midi. **d.** Tu te **rappelles** le dernier livre que tu as lu ? **e.** Elle lui **envoie** une lettre chaque semaine.

6 **a.** Tu **choisis** d'étudier l'anglais ? **b.** Nous **réussissons** toujours les examens d'histoire. **c.** Elle **maigrit** à vue d'œil ! **d.** Jacques **punit** souvent son fils. **e.** Vous ne **réfléchissez** pas assez !

7 **a.** Je **choisis** toujours la mauvaise caisse au supermarché! **b.** Nous **finissons** souvent avant le reste de la classe. **c.** Vous **bâtissez** une nouvelle maison ? **d.** Ils **réussissent** toujours à éviter de faire la vaisselle ! **e.** Tu **remplis** trop mon verre !

8 **a.** Tu **descends** au prochain arrêt ? **b.** Vous **perdez** toujours de l'argent au casino ! **c.** Sophie et Marc **vendent** de très jolies fleurs dans leur magasin. **d.** Nous **défendons** souvent notre sœur. **e.** Ils n'**entendent** pas la cloche de l'église !

9 **a.** Où **mets**-tu les sacs de voyage ? **b. Savez**-vous à quelle heure part le train ? **c.** Nous **voulons** voyager en avion cette fois-ci. **d. Peux**-tu porter cette valise, s'il te plaît ? **e.** Nous **devons** aller au terminal 1 ou au terminal 2 ? **f.** Je ne **vois** pas notre porte de départ !

10 **a.** Je **me** douche tous les matins. **b.** Elle **se** brosse les dents deux fois par jour. **c.** Nous **nous** lavons les mains constamment ! **d.** Vous **vous** rongez encore les ongles ! **e.** Ils **s'**habillent à 7h15 tous les jours.

11 **a. Écoute** le professeur ! **b.** Ne **regardez** pas par la fenêtre, mais **lisez** votre livre ! **c. Arrête** de parler avec ton voisin ! **d. Rendons** nos copies. Le test est terminé. **e. Prenez** vos livres et **ouvrez**-les à la page 47.

12 **a.** Apprends-le. **b.** Rangez-les. **c.** Prends-la. **d.** Éteignons-les. **e.** Accrochez-le.

11. Talking about the future

1 **a.** Je **mettrai** mon maillot de bain. **b.** Nous **descendrons** au restaurant. **c.** Le serveur nous **servira** notre cappuccino. **d.** Tu **mangeras** une salade de fruits frais. **e.** Nous nous **baignerons** dans l'océan turquoise.

2 **a.** Nous **danserons** toute la nuit ! **b.** Vous **choisirez** quoi comme vin, messieurs-dames ? **c. Prendras**-tu de l'eau ? **d.** Elles **chanteront** longtemps à la soirée karaoké. **e.** Il **rentrera** tard, c'est sûr !

3 **1.c.** L'**enverras**-tu à Stéphanie ? **2.b.** Que **ferons**-nous demain ? **3.a. Viendrez**-vous à nouveau l'année prochaine ? **4.b. Saurez**-vous retrouver la route ? **5.c.** Où **irons**-nous après le restaurant ?

4 **a.** [...], je **serai** à la plage ! **b.** Sandrine, **auras**-tu ton téléphone [...] ? **c.** Vous **verrez** ! [...] **d. Pourrons**-nous faire garder notre petite-fille ? **e.** Nos filles **iront** en excursion la semaine prochaine !

5 « Marie est très heureuse. Demain, Charles **arrivera** par le train, un bouquet à la main, prêt à l'épouser. Ils **se regarderont** et à cet instant précis, **se reconnaîtront**, pour la vie. [...] Ils **voyageront** autour du monde, **visiteront** tous ces pays dont ils ont parlé sans se lasser. Ils **pourront** parler sans interruption. Qui sait ? Ils se **marieront** ; **auront** des enfants, peut-être. Et **vivront** dans la paix,[...]. Ils **seront** ensemble, unis, contre tous. »

6 **a.** je vais **b.** tu vas **c.** il/elle va **d.** nous allons **e.** vous allez **f.** ils/elles vont

7 **a.** Nous **allons** voir le nouveau film ! **b. Allez**-vous assister au spectacle ? **c.** Je ne **vais** pas manger chez Chloé demain midi. **d.** Il **va** encore manger du chocolat en cachette ! **e.** Quand **vas**-tu aller poster les cartes de Noël ?

8 **a.** Dépêchez-vous ! Le spectacle **va commencer** ! **b.** Ta voiture est en panne ? Pas de problème ! Je **vais te conduire** au garage. **c.** Le ciel se couvre : je pense qu'il **va pleuvoir. d.** Les Lagrange **vont visiter** le Vietnam au mois d'août. **e. Allez-vous partir** en vacances cette année ?

9 **a.** Je **ne** vais **pas** suivre des cours à l'université. **b.** Julie **ne** va **pas** passer son permis de conduire la semaine prochaine. **c.** Elles **ne** vont **pas** se promener en ville cet après-midi. **d.** Vous **n'allez pas** rentrer à dix heures ce soir ? **e.** Tu **ne** vas **pas** rester à la maison demain ?

10 **a.** Je **partirai** quand Alexandre **arrivera**. **b.** Dorian **ira** chez son frère demain après-midi. **c.** Élise **sera** déçue lorsqu'elle **apprendra** que Corentin ne vient pas. **d.** Nous **viendrons** tous en vacances avec vous l'année prochaine ! **e.** Que **feras**-tu demain à cette heure-ci ?

12. The past and the conditional

1 **a.** nous partons → je partais **b.** nous aimons → ils aimaient **c.** nous croyons → tu croyais **d.** nous prenons → vous preniez **e.** nous faisons → elle faisait

2 **a.** Il **faisait** nuit lorsque l'avion a atterri. **b.** Nous **allions** à la plage tous les matins ! **c. Vouliez**-vous nous voir avant de partir ? **d.** Je **me sentais** très fatigué. **e.** Vous **habitiez** tous ensemble ? Vous **deviez** être à l'étroit ! ['cuisinait' n'est pas utilisé.]

3 **a.** Je **savais** que vous **étiez** en France ! **b.** Il **pensait** que tu **avais** deux chats ! **c.** Nous **avions** les cheveux blonds quand nous **étions** petits. **d.** **Mangeais**-tu des pâtes à 3 heures ce matin ? **e.** Avant, Caroline **appelait** sa sœur tous les soirs.

4	Passé composé	Imparfait
a. Je suis allée au théâtre.	✓	
b. Il préparait un gâteau au chocolat.		✓
c. Nous mangions au restaurant.		✓
d. Stéphane a vu un renard dans le pré.	✓	
e. Marie-Luce dormait à poings fermés.		✓
f. Gwendolyne s'est promenée au parc.	✓	
g. Vous avez regardé le film hier soir ?	✓	
h. Je lisais mon livre tranquillement.		✓

5 **a.** Je **faisais** la sieste lorsque la voisine **a sonné** à la porte. **b.** Lorsqu'il **est rentré**, Audrey **regardait** la télévision. **c.** Il **se rendait** à la banque quand il l'**a rencontrée**. **d.** Elles **étaient** en vacances et elles **ont acheté** de très jolis vêtements. **e.** Le chat **s'apprêtait** à bondir lorsque l'oiseau **s'est envolé**.

6 **1.e.** Je visitais l'Italie lorsque j'ai rencontré Lorenzo. **2.c.** Je garais la voiture quand la Peugeot m'est rentrée dedans ! **3.f.** Elle plantait de la menthe quand elle s'est fait piquer par une araignée. **4.b.** Passais-tu ton examen lorsque tu t'es évanouie ? **5.a.** Il redescendait la montagne quand il est tombé. **6.d.** Vous faisiez du ski lorsque vous vous êtes rencontrés ?

7 **a.** Je **partirais** en vacances demain ! **b.** Julian **finirait** sa toile s'il avait le temps ! **c.** Avec des « si » on **mettrait** Paris en bouteille ! **d.** Martine **préférerait** prendre le train. **e.** Hélène et Simon **vendraient** leur maison !

8 **a.** Si tu **parlais** moins, tu **finirais** plus vite ! **b.** Vous vous **amuseriez** vraiment si vous **veniez** en vacances ! **c.** Si Luc le lui **demandait**, Aline **aimerait** beaucoup l'épouser ! **d.** Nathan **serait** heureux si Julie lui **écrivait** une lettre.

9 **a.** Je **verrais** mieux si tu allumais la lumière ! **b.** Lucas **devrait** arrêter de courir. **c.** Il **faudrait** un miracle ! **d.** Il **gagnerait** la course. **e.** Louise **donnerait** tout ce qu'elle a pour une glace ! **f.** Nous **serions** déjà arrivés s'il n'y avait pas tant de circulation.

10 **a.** Je **préparais** le dîner lorsque Samuel **est arrivé**. **b.** Si tu **faisais** un effort, tu y **arriverais** ! **c.** Vous **verriez** la chenille si vous **regardiez** de plus près. **d.** Nous ne **pourrions** pas comprendre, même si nous **essayions**. **e.** J'**écoutais** la radio lorsque la nouvelle **est tombée**.

13. Prepositions

1 **a.** Anne et Marie se sont cachées **sous** la table ! **b.** Vas-tu **chez** tes parents **à** Pâques ? **c.** Edwige part **à** Tours **avec** ses enfants cet après-midi. **d.** Guy est allé **dans** la forêt cueillir des champignons. **e.** Elles sont parties **pendant** une heure.

2 **a.** Nous allons **au** Brésil le mois prochain ! **b.** Julien voudrait se rendre **en** Inde pour les vacances. **c.** Nadia vit **aux** Émirats Arabes Unis. **d.** Pablo est-il né **en** Espagne ou **au** Portugal ? **e.** J'adorerais passer Noël **aux** îles Fidji ! **f.** Kate retourne bientôt **en** Angleterre. **g.** Tu vas **à** Lille après-demain ?

3 **a.** Aden vit **à** Marrakech **au** Maroc. **b.** Acha vit **à** Yaoundé **au** Cameroun. **c.** Éléanore vit **à** Besançon **en** France. **d.** Aiko vit **à** Tokyo **au** Japon. **e.** Eeva vit **à** Helsinki **en** Finlande.

4 **a.** La balle est tombée **en bas des** escaliers. **b.** Le poulet est **dans** le frigo. **c.** Le chat de la voisine est coincé **en haut de** l'arbre ! **d.** Ton cochon d'Inde se cache encore **sous** le canapé [...] ! **e.** Pourquoi as-tu garé la voiture **devant** le garage [...] ?

5 **a.** Le restaurant est-il **loin** de la maison ? [...] **b.** La boulangerie se trouve **entre** la boucherie et le café. **c.** Les toilettes sont tout de suite **en haut** des escaliers [...]. **d.** Je crois que le gâteau est **sur** la table de la cuisine. **e.** [...] Il y a une énorme araignée **derrière** toi !

6 **a.** As-tu mis ma chemise **dans** le sac de voyage ? – Oui, elle est **dedans** ! **b.** Regarde ! Hélène est assise **à côté de** Sébastien ! **c.** Où est garée la moto ? – Elle est garée là, **à gauche.** **d.** Les clés sont **en dessous de** la valise. **e.** Oh non ! La maison est encore **loin** !

7 **a.** Je suis arrivé en retard **à l'**école ce matin. **b.** Vas-tu **à la** fête du village samedi prochain ? **c.** Ils sont allés **chez** Caroline hier soir. **d.** Stéphanie a rendez-vous **chez** le médecin vendredi matin à 9h30. **e.** Elles sont arrivées **aux** urgences vers minuit. **f.** Il vient d'arriver **au** bureau.

8 **1. Je vais :** à l'école. – à la pêche avec mon frère ! – au mariage de Maé et Joris. – aux vendanges !
2. Je sors de la boîte de nuit ! – du cours de guitare. – de l'opéra. – du cinéma.

9 **a.** Nous allons aller à la plage **pendant** les vacances ! **b.** Le train arrive **dans** une heure ! **c.** Il habite à Paris **depuis** 2002. **d.** La famille Charlet déménage **en** septembre. **e.** Ils parlent **pendant** des heures quand Jonathan téléphone ! **f.** Il fait beau **depuis** le milieu de l'été.

⑩

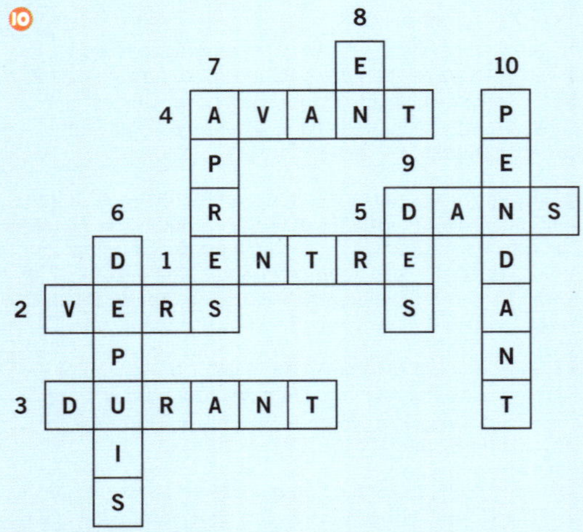

⑪ **1.f. au sujet de, à propos de** *about* **2.d. avec** *with* **3.c. contre** *against* **4.a. malgré** *in spite of* **5.h. par** *by* **6.b. quant à** *as for* **7.i. sans** *without* **8.e. sauf** *except* **9.g. selon** *according to*

⑫ **a.** Fais attention **aux** trous ! **b.** Julian joue **de la** guitare. **c.** Tu commences **à** comprendre cet exercice ! **d.** J'ai oublié **de** fermer la porte d'entrée ! **e.** Je me souviens **du** jour où la foudre est tombée sur ta maison !

14. Adverbs

① **a.** prudemment **b.** joliment **c.** malheureusement **d.** constamment **e.** gentiment **f.** joyeusement **g.** profondément

② **a.** Luc est tellement fatigué. **b.** Je ne vais pas souvent au théâtre. **c.** Il a beaucoup grandi cette année. **d.** Vous êtes très gentils. **e.** Il est entré silencieusement dans la maison.

③ **a.** C'est le **meilleur** film de l'année ! **b.** Louis m'a posé la question **gentiment**. **c.** Est-ce un **bon** dessert ? **d.** Vous allez **bien** ? **e.** Karine va beaucoup **mieux** aujourd'hui.

④ **a.** Je pars **souvent** en voyage. **b.** Je travaille **toujours** avec des enfants. **c.** Je travaille **parfois** avec un ordinateur. **d.** Je rencontre **souvent** des gens. **e.** Je bavarde **généralement** avec mes clients.

⑤ **a.** Il n'y va **jamais**. **b.** Elle n'y va que très **rarement**. **c.** Nous regardons **toujours** les programmes du soir ensemble ! **d.** Pas très **souvent**, mais **quelquefois** il y a un spectacle intéressant. **e.** Elle en sort **généralement** à 16h30.

⑥ **a.** Nous devons nous lever **tôt**. **b.** Des nuages sont apparus, **puis** le vent s'est levé. **c.** Rex ! Viens ici **tout de suite** ! Quelle bêtise as-tu encore faite ? **d.** Ne pleure pas Edwige, ta maman va rentrer **bientôt**. **e.** J'ai rencontré Carla **il y a** cinq ans et nous ne nous sommes pas quittés depuis ! **f.** Je viens **souvent** ici. **g.** J'en cuisine **rarement**.

⑦ **a.** Non, je l'ai cherché **partout** mais ne l'ai trouvé **nulle part**. **b.** Allez donc jouer **dehors** avec le ballon ! **c.** J'ai cherché Domino dehors et il était **à l'intérieur** ! **d.** Elle est **là-bas**, à côté des arbres ! Elle était vraiment **loin** ! **e.** Mais, je ne suis pas à l'étage, je suis **en bas** !

⑧ **a.** Il y a **trop de** sucre. **b.** Il y a **assez de** lait dans mon café. **c.** Il y avait très **peu de** gens présents. **d.** Oui, j'aimerais **plus de** sucre dans mon café, s'il vous plaît. **e.** Il y a **beaucoup de** gâteaux et ils sont tous appétissants !

⑨ **a. Où** est Thomas ? **b. Comment** es-tu allé à Dijon ? **c. Qui** est avec Florence ? **d. Quand** venez-vous nous voir ? **e. Pourquoi** es-tu en colère ?

⑩ **a.** Ma grand-mère conduit si **lentement** ! **b.** Il va **toujours / souvent** au travail en vélo. **c.** Tu as **probablement** raison. **d.** Je n'en mange **jamais**. **e. Malheureusement**, Jennifer et Océane ne pourront pas venir à ton anniversaire. **f.** Julien est **vraiment** très généreux. **g.** J'ai **bien** compris.

15. More on verbs

① **a. Devez**-vous aller à l'école demain ? **b.** Nous ne **pouvons** pas manger ou boire ici. **c. Puis**-je utiliser les toilettes, s'il vous plaît ? **d.** Elles **doivent** rentrer à 10 heures. **e.** Tu **veux** venir avec nous au cinéma ? **f.** Il **veut** visiter l'Écosse.

② **a.** Camille **peut** venir à la maison cet après-midi ? **b.** Vous **devez** ôter vos chaussures avant d'entrer. **c.** Je **dois** étudier pour cet examen ! **d.** Nous **devons** faire les courses pour le week-end. **e.** Elles **peuvent** nous entendre !

③ **1.d.** Sortez les skis ! Il neige ! **2.a.** Je dois trouver mon parapluie ! Il pleut ! **3.e.** Il faut mettre les manteaux ! Il fait froid ! **4.b.** Nous pouvons sortir en t-shirt ! Il fait beau ! **5.c.** Peux-tu me donner un verre d'eau ? Il fait chaud !

④ **a.** Il faut aller à l'école. **b.** Il fait très beau aujourd'hui ! **c.** C'est l'été ! Il fait très chaud. **d.** Il vaut mieux avoir un portable. **e.** Il n'y a pas beaucoup de monde / de gens ici.

⑤ **a.** Are you cold? **b.** I am very hungry. **c.** We are wrong. **d.** I am 41. **e.** You are lucky.

⑥ **a.** Tu as raison ! Il pleut ! **b.** J'ai vraiment froid ! Ferme la fenêtre ! **c.** Nous avons de la chance ! Nous avons gagné ! / On a gagné ! **d.** Quel âge a-t-elle ? – Elle a 26 ans. **e.** As-tu faim ?

⑦

Sentence	T	I
a. Nous mangeons une pizza tous les vendredis.	✓	
b. Sabine écoute une chanson.	✓	
c. Corinne parle à ses amis.		✓
d. Tu réponds à tante Colette ?		✓
e. Je bois du café tous les matins.	✓	

⑧

Sentence	D	I
a. J'ai donné mon livre.	✓	
b. Elle téléphone à Alice.		✓

c. Nous écrivons à nos parents.		✓
d. Tu chantes cette chanson.	✓	
e. Nous pensons à nos vacances.		✓

9 **a.** lançant **b.** aimant **c.** achetant **d.** voyant **e.** maigrissant **f.** venant **g.** s'habillant

16. Linking words

1 **a.** Je suis passé chez toi, mais tu n'étais pas là. **b.** Soit tu viens avec nous, soit tu ne viens pas [...] **c.** Marion pense cuisiner un bœuf bourguignon ou un navarin. **d.** La voiture est au garage donc je ne pourrai pas venir te voir ce matin. **e.** Je ne me sens pas très bien, cependant j'essaierai d'aller en cours.

2 **a.** Julien pose des questions **donc** il va falloir répondre. **b.** Laetitia n'aime pas skier, **c'est pourquoi** elle reste au chalet. **c.** Florian ne s'énerve jamais, **au contraire** il reste toujours serein. **d.** Marine n'aime pas le chocolat, **pourtant** elle a fait [...]. **e.** Maxime lui fait confiance, **cependant** il a un doute. **f.** Je suis au lit **car** je suis malade.

3 **a.** Claudette a pris un parapluie au cas où il pleuve. **b.** Bien que Pierre ait peur de l'eau, ils sont allés en vacances au bord de la mer. **c.** Comme les enfants n'aiment pas la télévision, j'ai apporté des jeux de société. **d.** Je partirai lorsque le film sera fini. **e.** Depuis que j'ai 18 ans, je me sens beaucoup plus libre !

4 **a.** aussitôt que = dès que **b.** comme = puisque **c.** lorsque = quand **d.** bien que = quoique

5 **a.** Depuis que je **suis** à la retraite, [...] ! **b.** Si tu **vas** en ville demain, préviens-moi ! **c.** Bien que les chiens me **fassent** peur, [...] ! **d.** Quand tu **arriveras,** [...]. **e.** Quoi que nous **disions,** [...].

6 **premièrement / d'abord / tout d'abord** *firstly* – **en premier lieu** *in the first place* – **deuxièmement** *secondly* – **ensuite / puis** *then*

7 **d'un côté... de l'autre** *on the one hand... on the other* – **d'une part... d'autre part...** *on the one hand... on the other* – **ou... ou...** *either... or* – **par ailleurs** *in addition* – **en outre** *moreover*

d'un autre côté *on the other hand* – **par contre** *on the other hand* – **en revanche** *in contrast* – **au contraire** *on the contrary*

8 **ainsi** *in this way* – **par exemple** *for example* – **notamment** *particularly* – **en particulier** *in particular*

9 **finalement / enfin** *finally* – **en conclusion / pour conclure** *to conlude* – **en résumé** *to summarize / to sum up* – **en bref** *in short* – **pour finir** *lastly*

10 **a. D'un côté**, tu pourrais penser [...], mais **de l'autre** [...]. **b.** Je n'aime pas certains gâteaux : **par exemple,** le mille-feuille [...]. **c. Premièrement**, j'aimerais présenter [...]. **d.** D'abord on travaille ; **ensuite** on s'amuse ! **e.** Elle a pris son parapluie ; elle sera **ainsi** protégée de la pluie.

17. The passive voice

1	**Active**	**Passive**
a. La vaisselle est faite par Joël.		✓
b. Catherine range le garage.	✓	
c. Le chat est brossé par Manon.		✓
d. Cette lettre est écrite par mon arrière-grand-mère !		✓
e. Mon père a peint cette toile.	✓	

2 **a.** Notre maison **est** construite [...]. **b.** Les haricots **sont** plantés par Julien. **c.** Nous **sommes** accueillis [...]. **d.** Vous **êtes** poursuivis [...] ! **e.** Tu **es** invitée par Ella.

3 **a.** Ces tartes **sont préparées** [...] **b.** L'arbre de Noël **est décoré** par les enfants. **c.** Le président français **est accueilli** par le premier ministre anglais. **d.** Les voleurs **sont arrêtés** par la police. **e.** Les commandes **sont prises** par la serveuse.

4 **a.** Cette sculpture **a été réalisée** [...]. **b.** Ce livre **a été écrit** [...]. **c.** La voiture **a été vendue** [...]. **d.** Ces crevettes **ont été préparées** [...]. **e.** Le ciel **a été illuminé** [...].

5 **a. On a réparé** le bateau. **b. On a changé** le numéro. **c. On a ouvert** le magasin. **d. On a cassé** le vase. **e. On a bâti** la maison.

6 **a.** Comment cela **se dit**-il en anglais ? **b.** Le vin blanc **se sert** très frais. **c.** Cela ne **se fait** pas. Ce n'est pas poli. **d.** Ce plat **se mange** chaud et accompagné de haricots blancs. **e.** Les toilettes **se trouvent** au fond du couloir.

7 **a.** Une pomme **a été mangée par** Caroline **b.** La Joconde **a été peinte par** Léonard de Vinci. **c.** Le ver de terre **a été mangé par** l'oiseau. **d.** Les jonquilles **ont été plantées** par Daniel. **e.** L'appartement **a été décoré par** Mathilde.

8	**Active**	**Passive**
Les cambrioleurs ont été surpris par les policiers.		✓
Notre président était respecté de tous.		✓
On interdit l'utilisation des téléphones portables dans la salle d'attente.	✓	
Ce fruit ne se mange pas.		✓
Karine est très appréciée de ses collègues.		✓

9 **Verb**	**Yes**	**No**
demander quelque chose à quelqu'un		✓
construire quelque chose pour quelqu'un	✓	
aller quelque part		✓
admirer par quelqu'un	✓	
promettre quelque chose à quelqu'un		✓
monter les escaliers		✓

manger quelque chose	✓	
tomber par terre		✓

18. The present subjunctive

1 **a.** Il faut que je **réussisse** [...]. **b.** [...] avant que Jean **vienne** me chercher. **c.** Pourvu que nous **vendions** [...]. **d.** [...] que tu **agrandisses** [...] ! **e.** [...] que tu **prennes** [...].

2 **a.** [...] que je **mange** [...]. **b.** [...] que tu **écoutes** la radio. **c.** [...] qu'elle **maigrisse** très vite. **d.** [...] que nous **mettions** la table. **e.** [...] que vous **perdiez** [...]. **f.** [...] qu'ils **choisissent** toujours les bonnes cartes.

3 **a.** [...] que tu **sois** [...]. **b.** [...] que nous **soyons** [...]. **c.** que vous **soyez** à l'heure. **d.** [...] que je **sois** [...]. **e.** [...] qu'elle **soit** [...]. **f.** Bien qu'ils **soient** [...].

4 **a.** Bien que je n'**aie** [...]. **b.** Il faut que tu **aies** [...]. **c.** [...] qu'elle **ait** [...]. **d.** [...] qu'ils **aient** [...]. **e.** [...] que vous **ayez** [...]. **f.** [...] que nous **ayons** [...].

5 **a.** [...] que vous **veniez** [...]. **b.** [...] que tu **saches** [...]. **c.** [...] que tu **fasses** [...]. **d.** [...] que vous **deviez** [...]. **e.** [...] que ton père **prenne** [...]. **f.** [...] que tu **ailles** [...].

6 **a.** [...] que vous **buviez** [...] ! **b.** [...] qu'ils **aillent** [...]. **c.** [...] que tu **reçoives** [...]. **d.** [...] que tu **tiennes** [...]. **e.** [...] que vous **fassiez** [...].

7 **a.** Je viendrai samedi, **à moins que** [...]. **b.** Je t'ai apporté cette couverture **pour que** [...]. **c. Bien que** je n'aime pas [...]. **d. Pourvu qu'**il ne vienne pas [...]. **e.** Je continuerai les leçons **jusqu'à ce que** [...].

8 **a.** [...] que nous **gagnions** [...]. **b.** [...] que tu **viennes** [...]. **c.** [...] que vous **finissiez** [...]. **d.** [...] que tu **veuilles** [...]. **e.** [...] que vous **ayez** [...].

9 **a. Il est impossible que** j'aie perdu [...]. **b. Il est probable qu'**il y ait [...]. **c. Il est possible que** nous soyons sélectionnés [...]. **d. Il se peut que** ma jambe soit cassée. **e. Il est douteux que** j'aie la rubéole.

10 **a.** Il serait étonnant que je **reçoive** [...]. **b.** C'est dommage que tu ne **boives** pas de cidre. **c.** Il vaut mieux que nous **allions** au cinéma [...]. **d.** C'est bizarre que tu **aies** un chien [...]. **e.** Il faut que nous **rendions** nos livres [...].

11 **a.** C'est le meilleur film que j'**aie** jamais vu ! **b. Où que** tu ailles [...]. **c. Quoi que** tu fasses [...]. **d.** Je ne crois pas qu'il **soit** [...]. **e.** Je ne pense pas qu'il **mange** de viande.

19. The past historic

1 Il était une fois un meunier qui, lorsqu'il **mourut**, **légua** tous ses biens à ses trois fils. L'aîné **hérita** d'un moulin, le cadet d'un âne, et le plus jeune, Paul, d'un chat. « Lorsque je l'aurai mangé, **soupira**-t-il, il ne me restera plus qu'à mourir de faim ! » Mais le chat l'**entendit** et **prépara** un plan : [...] Paul était sceptique, mais **fit** ce que le chat lui demandait : « Aussi, si quelqu'un vous le demande, vous vous appelez désormais monsieur le Marquis de Carabas », **ajouta** le chat. Le chat **mit** de la nourriture dans son sac et **s'allongea** sur le sol, comme mort.

2 **a.** La réunion **débuta** à 10 heures. **b.** Clément et Zoé **arrivèrent** à l'aéroport à l'heure. **c.** Nous **attendîmes** pendant des heures. La tension **monta**. **d.** Vous **partîtes**. La maison **sembla** vide. **e.** Je **pris** beaucoup de photos.

3 **a.** Elles **eurent** soudain très soif. **b.** Nous **eûmes** l'idée d'aller au cinéma tous ensemble. **c.** Lorsqu'elle ouvrit la fenêtre, j'**eus** très froid. **d.** Il **eut** une peur bleue lorsque la foudre tomba sur la maison voisine ! **e.** Ils **eurent** beaucoup de difficultés à organiser ce voyage.

4 **a.** Ils **furent** les premiers soldats américains à Paris. **b.** Nous **fûmes** très surpris. **c.** Louis de Funès **fut** très célèbre dans les années 1970 **d.** Tu **fus** un des élèves les plus populaires du lycée. **e.** Vous **fûtes** très heureux de réussir votre examen.

5 Le Petit Poucet **dut** se lever de bon matin et **prit** le chemin du ruisseau. Il emplit ses poches de petits cailloux blancs et **revint** ensuite à la maison. Il **alla** dans une forêt dense. Le bûcheron **se mit** à couper du bois et les enfants ramassèrent des brindilles. Lorsque les parents **virent** que les enfants étaient occupés, ils s'enfuirent rapidement. Le Petit Poucet **courut** partout pour retrouver ses parents mais **dut** renoncer, tristement.

6 **a.** Elle **mit** sa robe rapidement pour ne pas être en retard. **b.** Ils **reconnurent** le bandit et lui **coururent** après. **c.** Je **sus** immédiatement que quelque chose lui était arrivé. **d.** Nous **allâmes** au restaurant après la cérémonie. **e.** Tu **fus obligée de** prendre le train plus tard que prévu suite aux intempéries.

7 **a.** Ils **avancèrent** dans la neige avec difficulté. **b.** Nous **voyageâmes** pendant deux mois ! **c.** Il **neigea** toute la journée. **d.** Vous **commençâtes** la réunion sans Romain. **e.** Martin **remplaça** David qui était malade. **f.** Vous **nageâtes** pendant deux heures !

8

			1								
		5	H	U	R	L	A				4
			A								R
		6	B	Û	M	E	S				E
			I			2			3		M
7	F	A	L	L	U	T			F		P
			L			Î			I		L
			A			N			N		A
			I			M			I		Ç
				8	R	E	G	A	R	D	A
						S			E		
									N		
9	P	L	A	C	È	R	E	N	T		

9 Il était une fois une petite poule rousse qui **sortit** de chez elle pour aller en ville. Elle **mit** la clé dans sa poche mais sa poche avait un trou et la clé **tomba** par terre. La petite poule ne le **vit** pas et **poursuivit** son chemin. Maître Renard **apparut**. Il n'avait qu'une envie : manger la poulette ! Lorsqu'il **aperçut** la clé sur le sol, il la **ramassa** et **courut** ouvrir la porte de la maisonnette.

20. Review

1 **a.** J'ai **le** cafard. **b.** Tu me casses **les** oreilles ! **c.** Il m'a posé **un** lapin ! **d.** C'est **la** fin **des** haricots ! **e.** Arrête de faire **l'**andouille !

2 **a. un professeur** *a teacher / lecturer / professor* **b. un chanteur** *a singer* **c. une vendeuse** *a shop assistant* (fem.) **d. un médecin** *a doctor* **e. un ingénieur** *an engineer* **f. un serveur** *a waiter* **g. un concierge** *a caretaker* **h. un boulanger** *a baker*

3 **a. est** = être (others: avoir) **b. étant** = present participle (others: past participles) **c. je** = subject pronoun (others: object pronouns) **d. Mexique** = country (others = nationalities) **e. chat** = animal (others = colours)

4

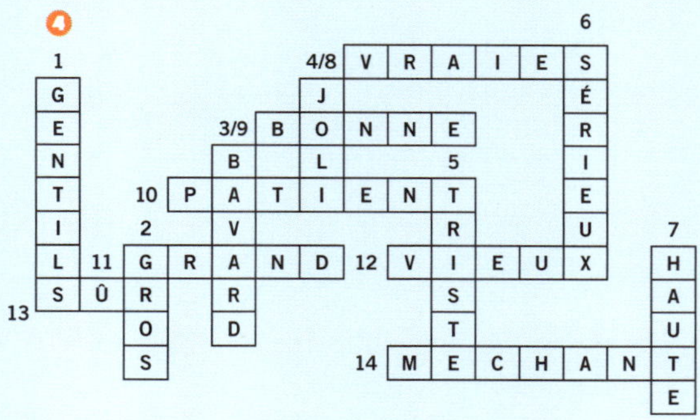

5 **a.** Quentin est allé au cinéma avec ses amis.
b. Je pense faire un grand voyage l'année prochaine.
c. Ils organiseront une fête d'anniversaire pour Marion.
d. Je faisais la sieste lorsque tu as frappé à la porte.
e. Eva commencera le travail dès son retour.

6	**Present**	**Perfect**
regarder	je regarde	**j'ai regardé**
faire	**tu fais**	**tu as fait**
vendre	il vend	**il a vendu**
finir	**nous finissons**	nous avons fini
boire	**vous buvez**	**vous avez bu**
aller	elles vont	**elles sont allées**

Future	**Conditional**	**Imperfect**
je regarderai	**je regarderais**	**je regardais**
tu feras	**tu ferais**	tu faisais
il vendra	il vendrait	**il vendait**
nous finirons	**nous finirions**	**nous finissions**
vous boirez	**vous boiriez**	vous buviez
elles iront	elles iraient	**elles allaient**

7 01:30 = Il est une heure trente.

04:30 = Il est quatre heures et demie.

10:45 = Il est onze heures moins le quart.

02:15 = Il est deux heures et quart.

12:00 = Il est midi.

07:50 = Il est huit heures moins dix.

03:25 = Il est trois heures vingt-cinq.

8			A	C	O	M	M	E	P
			I					L	O
			N					O	U
Q			S	C				R	R
	U		I			A		S	T
	Q	O		D			R	Q	A
	U		I		O			U	N
	A			Q		N		E	T
M	N				U		C		
A	D					E			
I	T	O	U	T	E	F	O	I	S
S				A	U	S	S	I	
N	E	A	N	M	O	I	N	S	

9 **a.** J'ai rêvé que je gagnais au loto ! **b.** Il a été au cinéma hier. **c.** Vous avez aimé ma tarte aux pommes ? **d.** Tu as compris l'exercice de grammaire ? **e.** Nous sommes partis à 8 heures.

10 **a.** 46 = quarante-six **b.** 99 = quatre-vingt-dix-neuf **c.** 318 = trois cent dix-huit **d.** 72 = soixante-douze **e.** 502 cinq cent deux **f.** 152 = cent cinquante-deux **g.** 1008 = mille huit **h.** 683 = six cent quatre-vingt-trois

Illustration credits

Shutterstock : Aleutie : pp. 77b ; 84h ; Akai37 : p. 4 ; Ankomando : pp. 7d ; 101g ; Ann Doronina : p. 98h ; Anthony Krikorian : p. 79h ; A-R-T : p. 73 ; BoBaa22 : p. 63b ; COCOart : p. 107d ; dedMazay : p. 113d ; D.J.McGee : p. 94d ; Gamegfx : p. 22h ; HappyJack : p. 43b ; Inni : p. 62h ; iNueng : p. 89mg ; Jesadaphorn : p. 78 ; Julie A. Felton : p. 89hd ; Julia Tim : p. 88b ; Iamnee : p. 96b ; Kyuree : p. 72b ; Mackey Creations : p. 16bd ; Maglara : p. 55 ; Marish : pp. 63h ; 70b ; NatBasil : p. 59b ; Nikita Chisnikov : p. 47 ; Paper Teo : p. 58b ; Ramona Kaulitzki : p. 111h ; Sentavio : p. 68bg ; Serbinka : p. 90hg ; sir.Enity : p. 73h ; Smart Design : p. 59h ; Stella Levi : p. 95h ; Stockshoppe : pp. 87bg ; 87bd ; subarashii21 : p. 3 ; venimo : pp. 16g ; 94g ; Viktorija Reuta : p. 60b ; Vitamind : p. 76h ; VooDoo13 : p. 53d ; whanwhan.ai : p. 52 - Droits réservés : pp. 5 ; 7g ; 8h ; 8b ; 9h ; 9b ; 10h ; 10b ; 11h ; 11m ; 11b ; 12 ; 13 ; 14 ; 15 ; 16hd ; 17 ; 19 ; 20 ; 21 ; 22b ; 23 ; 24 ; 25 ; 26 ; 27 ; 28 ; 29 ; 30 ; 31 ; 32 ; 33 ; 34 ; 35 ; 36 ; 37 ; 38 ; 39 ; 40 ; 41 ; 43h ; 44 ; 45 ; 46 ; 48 ; 49 ; 50 ; 51 ; 53g ; 54 ; 56 ; 58h ; 60h ; 61 ; 62b ; 64 ; 65 ; 66 ; 67 ; 68bd ; 68m ; 68hd ; 68 hg ; 69 ; 70h ; 71 ; 72h ; 74 ; 73m ; 73b ; 76m ; 76b ; 77m ; 77h ; 79m ; 79h ; 80 ; 81 ; 82 ; 83 ; 84b ; 85 ; 86 ; 87h ; 88h ; 88m ; 89bd ; 90hd ; 90bg ; 90bd ; 91 ; 92 ; 93 ; 95b ; 96h ; 97 ; 98b ; 99 ; 100 ; 101d ; 102 ; 103 ; 104 ; 105 ; 106 ; 107g ; 108 ; 109 ; 110 ; 111b ; 112 ; 113g ; 114 ; 116 ; 117 ; 119.

Félicitations ! You've reached the end of this workbook! Now it's time to assess how you did by counting up the icons of each type for all the lessons. Make sure that you've put the sub-totals from each lesson in the boxes below, then add them up to find the total number for each of the three icons.

Lesson			
1. Alphabet and pronunciation			
2. Articles and nouns			
3. Pronouns			
4. Adjectives			
5. Comparatives and superlatives			
6. Sentences and word order			
7. More on pronouns			
8. Numbers and time			
9. Verbs & the perfect tense			
10. Talking about the present			
11. Talking about the future			
12. The past and the conditional			
13. Prepositions			
14. Adverbs			
15. More on verbs			
16. Linking words			
17. The passive voice			
18. The present subjunctive			
19. The past historic			
20. Review			
Total (all lessons)			

Which icon has the highest total?

Bravo ! You have mastered the basics of French and are now ready to move on to the next level!

Pas mal du tout...
but there is room for improvement. Go back and redo the exercises that gave you trouble, reviewing the information if necessary.

Encore un petit effort !
You're a bit rusty ... Go through the workbook again and redo the exercises, reviewing the information first.

Designed by: MediaSarbacane
Layout: Aurélia Monnier for Céladon Editions
Production: Céladon Editions

Publication number: 4358 - October 2024
ISBN: 978-2-7005-8151-5
www.assimil.com
Printed in Romania by Master Print